PICKING
COTTON

PICKING

OUR MEMOIR OF INJUSTICE AND REDEMPTION

COTTON

JENNIFER THOMPSON-CANNINO

AND RONALD COTTON

WITH ERIN TORNEO

ST. MARTIN'S PRESS ▧ NEW YORK

Note to the Reader

The names and identifying details of some individuals in this book have been changed. For information regarding sources, please see the notes at the end of the book.

www.stmartins.com

Library of Congress Cataloging-in-Publication Data

Thompson-Cannino, Jennifer.
    Picking Cotton : our memoir of injustice and redemption / Jennifer Thompson-Cannino and Ronald Cotton with Erin Torneo.—1st ed.
        p. cm.
    ISBN-13: 978-0-312-37653-6
    ISBN-10: 0-312-37653-7
    1. Thompson-Cannino, Jennifer. 2. Rape victims—North Carolina—Burlington—Biography. 3. Rape—North Carolina—Burlington—Case studies. 4. Cotton, Ronald. 5. Forgiveness—Case studies. I. Cotton, Ronald. II. Torneo, Erin. III. Title.
    HV6568.B87T56 2009
    362.883092'2756—dc22
    [B]

2008035449

First Edition: March 2009

10   9   8   7   6   5   4   3   2   1

For all those whose voices may never be heard—
the victims—on both sides of wrongful convictions

Prologue

RONALD COTTON stands a few rows behind Jennifer Thompson-Cannino, watching as she cranes her head through the crowd, looking for him among the faces of the parents who have come out to watch their children play soccer. All of the fields at Northeast Park in Gibsonville, North Carolina, are occupied on this bright autumn afternoon: It's tournament day, with a parking lot crammed full of yellow school buses, SUVs, and station wagons to prove it.

"Where are you?" she says into her cell phone, unable to find him.

"I'm right here," Ron says, enjoying the joke. Then he reaches out and touches Jennifer's arm, causing her to turn and jump.

"It's so good to see you," she says, laughing and moving close to embrace him. "You'd think I would've spotted you!" Wearing a blue baseball hat, Ron at six foot four towers over her. He's got to lean *waay* down to hug Jennifer, a tiny blonde with bobbed hair. The sun catches the sterling medallion he always wears around his neck: an eagle in flight.

Ron immediately gets into the game. "C'mon! Don't let 'em take that ball!" he shouts, clapping his hands.

Beside him, Raven, his nine-year-old daughter in neat braids he helped do that morning, shoots him a look. "Daddy!"

"What? Am I embarrassing you?" She nods, which only makes Ron yell louder. "Let's go!"

He is cheering on Jennifer's sixteen-year-old daughter, Brittany, who plays center-midfield, the link between offense and defense. Her brown ponytail bopping behind her, she keeps her cleats close to the ball, switch-backing across the field to try to keep it away from the other side until she's got a clear path to pass it to her fellow players. When she sees her opening, Brittany makes a strong, sure kick and sends the ball to her teammate, who takes off for the goal. The crowd yells for the black and white ball to make it into the net as if nothing could matter more.

The Reds, Brittany's team, win the first game of the tournament, and then they break for lunch. Brittany, spotting Ron and Raven with her mom, jogs over and hugs them both, happy they are there. The four of them head over with the other parents to the park's pavilion. With his Burger King bags picked up from the drive-in, Ron isn't part of the usual soccer parent crowd: moms like Jennifer who unpack neatly prepared sandwiches and snacks from Tupperware and coolers. After the kids eat, Brittany heads off to the grass to show Raven how to kick straight and dribble, while Jennifer and Ron catch up. One nosy mom can't resist and comes over to say hello.

"Jennifer, Brittany was just great today!" she says. "Too bad your husband missed it. Where is he?"

"He's with my son, doing 'guy stuff,' but they should be here any minute," says Jennifer.

The mother's eyes dart over to Ron and back to Jennifer. She can't figure it out. "So how do y'all know each other?" the mom says, motioning to Ron.

Jennifer and Ron look at each other, smiling. They let the moment settle between them, hanging in the air like the sweet green smell of freshly cut grass, ready for hordes of high school girls to trample it.

"We go way back," Ron says, in his characteristic way of understating things.

What they don't say is that twenty-two years ago, Jennifer sat in a jailhouse just five miles down the interstate, looked at seven black men standing in front of her, and picked Ronald Cotton as the man who had brutally raped her eleven days before.

Conquered they can never be
whose spirits and whose souls are free.

———————

—*Inscription on the Confederate Soldier statue
outside the Alamance County Courthouse
where Ronald Cotton was convicted*

PART 1

Jennifer

CHAPTER 1

I USED TO WALK three miles to campus and back every day from my apartment in Burlington. There weren't any sidewalks on West Front Street, so during the summer I hugged the edge of the road, trying to stay in the patches of shade when the magnolia trees provided them. I didn't know many people in my neighborhood, although I passed their houses and proud lawns every day. I don't know if I ever even noticed the brick home with white trim just beyond my apartment complex, but on the night that I ran through the damp grass, wearing only a blanket, it was that door I pounded on.

On my way to school, my head was always buried in index cards. I had stacks and stacks of them, careful notes all hole punched and ring bound—a different ring for every class. Just across from campus was a Hardee's, where I'd stop and get a coffee, then sit outside and keep studying. I didn't look over my shoulder or pay too much attention. My focus was on what lay ahead: I was going to graduate in the fall with a perfect 4.0, and my boyfriend, Paul, and I were talking about getting married. He was in his first year of business school at UNC–Chapel Hill. That's all my life was really about: college and my boyfriend. I was twenty-two years old and those were the kind of crystal-clear pictures I carried in my mind.

One night coming home in the dark—it must have been the beginning of July—I noticed a small orange glow as I was walking up to my door. It was just a pinprick of light cutting through the branches. The dry burn caught in the back of my throat. In the tree across from my bedroom window, someone was smoking a cigarette. I couldn't see who it was, but someone was there. I told myself it must be a kid—someone who had climbed up the tree to sneak a smoke. I gave it no further thought.

But that's the picture that flashed in my mind afterward, a snapshot uncovered by my brain as it was reeling for answers to what happened later that month—July 1984.

• • •

Burlington, North Carolina, is like most college towns: It swells during the school year with kids from Elon College, and contracts during the summer, when many of them return to their hometowns, to their parents, to the summer jobs they've had since they were in high school. I'd decided to stay that summer because I was taking classes, and because Paul was from Burlington, and would be home for the summer break from his classes in Chapel Hill. His parents ran a barbecue place in downtown, or what was left of it. Already the little mom-and-pop stores were emptying out or moving closer to the newly built mall near Huffman Mill Road, right off of I-40. But people still came to J.J.'s BBQ no matter what. They came for the vinegared pork and sweet tea that were as much a part of the Burlington summer as the humidity.

Most days I taught aerobics at Spa Lady, and on Saturdays, when I finished teaching, I would stay to lift some weights and put in a few hours at the sales desk. That Saturday was no different. When I got off, Paul and I spent the afternoon together, browsing at a shopping mall and eating lunch nearby until the heat finally got to us. We ended up back at my apartment, napping in the comfort of the air-conditioning. In the early evening, it cooled off enough for us to play tennis at the Alamance County Country Club, where he and his family were members. We were famished when we finished our showers, so we headed over to China Inn Restaurant—a favorite of ours. It was one of those all-you-can-eat deals, and I loaded up on fried rice, spring rolls, and refill after refill of sweet iced tea. I'm sure all the MSG had something to do with it—by the time we got to his friend's party, a fierce headache was blooming behind my eyes. We didn't stay very long.

Back at my apartment we turned up the A/C unit in the den full blast. Paul came into my room, carrying a glass of water and some aspirin. I fell asleep to his rubbing my back. The police report would later indicate that he slipped out around 11:00 P.M., taking care not to wake me.

• • •

Around 3:00 A.M., something pulled me from sleep, the sound of feet shuffling. At the twilight edge of consciousness, I searched the dim borders between sleep and wakefulness. Was it a noise from my dream? A nightmare? Or something outside my head? All I heard was the thrum and rattle of the air conditioner against the metal frame of the window. My weighted eyelids closed and sank me right back into sleep.

Something grazed my arm. I opened my eyes and felt my heart hammering through my chest. Everything was still and quiet, save for the percussion of blood in my ears, the rush of my breath. My body was terrified although my mind hadn't caught up yet. I struggled to focus my eyes in the fuzzy dark of my room. Instinctively, I pulled the sheets up around my neck. I began to make out the contours of my white dresser, my Smurfette doll, the pale blue and peach knickknacks my mom and I had cheerily decorated the apartment with when I'd moved in the previous fall. By the side of my bed, as I made out an unfamiliar roundness, a stab of pure panic hit my gut. It was the top of someone's head. Somebody was crouching by my right side.

"Who is that? Who's there?" I said, allowing myself to think it must be Paul, or someone playing a stupid joke.

A man sprang up and was on me in seconds. I heard myself scream. Something cold, flat, and metallic pressed into my neck. My mind snapped awake.

"Shut up or I'll cut you!" he hissed, clamping a gloved hand down over my mouth. His breath was inches from my own, and it reeked like an old ashtray someone had spilled beer all over.

Can't breathe, I tried to say, my words muffled by the rough material of his glove. He moved his hand away from my mouth and used it to pin my arms back over my head. "Scream and I'll kill you," he said, pushing the point of the blade harder into my neck with his other hand. My first thought was that he was robbing me and that, when I woke up, I'd startled him. I told him he didn't have to hurt me. I would give him my credit cards, my car keys. I would not call the police.

"My wallet is in the den," I offered, my voice strangled and small from the lack of air in my constricted chest. "Take all my money." I squirmed under him but he was too heavy, the lamp on my night table too far out of my reach. Without anything to use as a weapon, I had little to help me fight back. I was certain that even if I freed my hands, the best I could do was slap him before he stabbed me. I couldn't kick him because he was sitting on my legs. At five foot two, I knew I wouldn't win a physical struggle.

There in my memory, at the knife-edge of fear, time distorted: Some moments hurtled by; others seeped by slowly, as if they were becoming one with everything I was ever going to be. In this particular moment, he sneered at me.

"I got your ten dollars," he said, "but I don't want your fucking money." He reached down, yanked the sheet away from me, and pulled off my purple underwear.

The definitiveness of that knowledge—that I was going to be raped—settled on me like his weight, crushing me. *Was this how I was going to die? Was this the last thing I would see?* My head ran its own track of protest while my body lay there, unable to move. *I don't want to die! I want to live! I want to see my mom and dad again! Paul!*

"Just relax. It's been a long time for you, hasn't it, baby?" He put his head down between my legs. The intimacy of this gesture revolted me. My body went rigid, an unconscious resistance all the way down to the muscle: *Don't touch me.* The Chinese food

I'd eaten with Paul churned in my stomach. Was it only a few hours ago that we'd sat at China Inn? My disbelief was a kind of vertigo, and I clutched dumbly for anything to prove that this wasn't really happening. But those hours were already part of something else that seemed to drift further and further out of reach: before—a perpetual yesterday before this night ripped a hole in my life that I tumbled into, bottomless and dark. I swallowed back my nausea, grateful that all I had drunk at dinner was iced tea. It seemed vital that my mind was clear because I was imploring it to figure out what to do. *Think. Think!* My mind wanted to leave, to dull the sensate horror of his hands and mouth on me, but I knew I must stay present if I was going to have any chance of staying alive.

"Your man's overseas in Germany, ain't he?" He was wrong. It was my brother Joe who was backpacking over there, but I didn't bother to correct him. He took my stunned silence for what it was, interpreted it. "I know all about you, Jennifer. You from Winston-Salem. They burned witches there, ain't that right?" he said. "Yeah, you a witch. We gonna have a good time tonight."

Again I didn't correct him, but I registered that he wasn't as smart as he thought. In school, we had studied the Salem witch trials in Massachusetts, and I never forgot Giles Corey, the only man in American history ever pressed to death. To force him to talk, the court had placed a board upon his chest and piled on stone after stone. His last words were, "More weight," before his lungs collapsed and his rib cage snapped all around him.

My bones didn't give way. I was alive and breathing, alert to the sounds of his unzipping and kicking off his shoes and my silent dread of anticipating what was next. I smelled the scent of cigarette smoke all over him and then he was inside me, his face just above mine. He told me he knew I wore glasses, so he thought I couldn't see him. He was wrong again. My glasses were for distance; everything right in front of me, I could see. Light from the parking lot lamppost filtered through the blinds—it wasn't a lot but it was enough. In blinks, I willed myself to note the details. I studied his face for features to identify. The hairline, his awful mouth. Did he have scars? Tattoos? He had close-cropped hair. Although I didn't want to look at him, I had to. How much could I bear?

I tried to look in his eyes. They were distinctly almond shaped, small, and set deep into his face. I searched for something human to connect to, some kind of appeal I could make through eye contact. But he kept shifting his dark gaze from my eyes. He had high, broad cheekbones, and his mouth was not overly large. A faint shadow of hair framed his upper lip; it looked more like dirt than a mustache.

He kept talking to me, telling me I probably never had a man like him. It was sick what he did, as if we were lovers meeting surreptitiously in the middle of the night, as if this was some kind of fantasy. I was never so enraged and frightened at the same time. My hands balled up into fists—I couldn't stop the fight in them, useless as they were under him. I thought if I could just keep him talking, if I could win his trust, maybe I could get him to put his weapon down. Maybe I could figure out a way to run. I was trying to learn anything about where he lived, or went to school, how old he was, any clue to who this monster in the dark was. The only way I could fight him was to outsmart him.

"I'm afraid of knives," I told him. "I can't relax until you put it down. Can you put it outside? On my car?" I lied. But it was all a twisted lie anyway: his kissing me, talking to me. Like it was a game we were playing together.

I could sense his giving in. He stopped and looked at me. "You ain't gonna call the police?" Here it was: my will staking a claim, this first tiny victory giving way to a hope that maybe I would survive the night.

"No. Just drop it outside on my car. Please, I can't relax." I used his words. He didn't get angrier. If he did this, I thought, I could shut the door behind him fast. It'll give me enough time to call 911. I had no way of knowing that the phone lines had already been cut.

He began to get off me. He reached for his shoes on the floor, the ones he'd removed as he got on me, punctuating the moment with a thud. They were black canvas shoes. He moved slowly, testing me, unsure. I didn't feel powerful, but we were at least negotiating now. His uncertainty about what I was going to do reminded me that he hadn't taken everything from me.

"I have to pee," I announced. I wasn't asking for his permission. I headed out to the hallway, toward the bathroom. "First, I have to watch you go outside so I know you really went. While you're out there, I'll go to the bathroom." I grabbed the soft stadium blanket and wrapped it around me—Hennie, our housekeeper, my second mother, gave this to me—the red, yellow, and blue plaid that I was hoping, wishing, and praying would keep him from touching me again. I trembled with fear and he accepted it was because I was cold. But the blanket was a deliberate choice. I wasn't wearing any clothes, but that wasn't going to stop me from running if I got a chance. Once in the bathroom, I turned on the light, getting another glimpse of his face.

"Turn it off!" he yelled, retreating like a wounded animal into the shadows. I closed the door and ran the water. The bathroom window was too small for me to climb out; if he came after me in here, I'd be trapped. I rushed out into the hallway.

There was a night-light in the den, breaking up the inky corners of the hallway. My eyes continued to adjust to the dark, giving me more detail on him. Standing next to him for a few minutes, I tried to record information about how tall he was, if he walked pigeon toed or duck footed. Based on my height, I figured he must be about six feet tall. As he inched his way toward the front door, he didn't take his eyes off me. "You gonna let me back in, right?"

I reassured him, did my best to sound natural. But I frantically wondered if I could be fast enough to get to the front door before he came back in. It was a chance I'd have to take. I heard the knife hit the table on the porch, his frame still in the doorway. He never even stepped outside; in an instant, he shut and locked the front door. I remained in the hallway, moving toward the den—anything to keep from going back into the bedroom with him. I needed a new plan.

"Turn on the stereo," he commanded. I walked into the living room, and I saw my postcards and pictures scattered all over the coffee table. I hit the power button on the radio, the DJ's voice on KISS coming through the speakers. I needed to get to the back door. Maybe it was open.

"I'm thirsty. I'm gonna get a drink. You want something?" Another stalling tactic I hoped would buy me some time.

He fiddled with the dial, and the blue LCD light illuminated his profile as he trolled for a station. He didn't have a wide nose.

"Yeah, fix me something with Seagram's and let's make it a party."
Then he held up something.

"Can I have this?" he said. It was a picture of me, standing in a
bathing suit at Apex Lake. Why he asked me this still baffles me,
since permission was so beside the point. I nodded and he put it in
his back pocket.

I headed into the kitchen. If I survived, I told myself, I would
tell the police he was a light-skinned black man, wearing dark
khakis, a blue shirt with white stripes on the sleeve, and canvas
boat shoes. He wore white knit gloves on his hands. I still had the
fibrous taste of them in my mouth.

I flipped on the light switch, because I knew it would protect
me. It was a small buffer zone: he wouldn't come too close to me
with the light on. On the table I saw a pack of Vantage cigarettes
from my purse, empty Coors cans, my wallet with my license out.
How long was he here while I slept?

Maybe only fifteen feet were between us, but he was behind a
corner, just out of sight. I turned on the faucet. The water hitting
the basin made a loud, tinny sound. I opened the cupboards,
clanked glasses together, threw ice cubes in the sink. I zeroed in
on the door in my kitchen. His way in was my only way out. I
heard his voice coming toward the kitchen. "Is that door locked?"
he yelled. *Run!*

I set out in my backyard. It was misting rain, and the grass was
wet and cool under my feet. I headed immediately to the right—
the next unit. I banged on my neighbor's back door, screaming.
But there was no time to waste. No time for someone sleeping to
hear me, get out of bed, and open the door. He was already coming out my door. I ran across the yard to the next building. I

didn't have any plan other than to run. He was somewhere behind me in pursuit, but the soft, damp ground absorbed the sound of his and my footsteps. A tree branch whipped me in the face, and I staggered into a corner between two buildings that connected in a L-shape, a place that had no escape if he found me. Out of the corner of my eye I saw a light on—in a brick house with a carport. I hopped the low dog fence that separated that property from the apartment complex, and slammed my hands on the screen door, frantically hitting the doorbell. I knew my stalker could see me in the light. *Please open. Please open.*

A man inside the house saw me through the window of the door. "Help me, please! I've been raped by a black man! He's after me!" I yelled. The man screamed. Behind him, his wife appeared. "She's a student at the college. I recognize her. Let her in." As their door locked behind me, I fainted. Everything went black as I saw the terror in this man's eyes of what the night had brought him. This hysterical girl, naked except for a blanket. When I came to, I heard them calling 911. All the lights were off, but we could see my rapist circling the house. The man who let me in stood by the door with a baseball bat.

· · ·

Here is where there are moments lost forever down in that black hole, gaps of time I must have lived through but have no recollection of. The moments that remain are fragments: hard, sharp fragments. Somehow I was then in the back of an ambulance. I heard the sirens and the bloodhounds. The drag of the windshield wipers back and forth across the glass, clearing the fine coating of rain.

At Memorial Hospital, when I was told to undress, I realized that I was not wearing my own clothes. The plaid blanket was gone. I now wore green athletic shorts, someone else's underwear, and a T-shirt. The people who had let me in must have given me some of their teenaged daughter's clothing. I was aware of the material touching my body, only it no longer felt like my body. I was no longer me. The girl in my mind, the picture-perfect student who would be getting married soon to Paul, was sucked down by that black hole, too.

The doctor was called in, sleep still in his eyes. He didn't look too happy about being awakened in the middle of the night. And it was clearly my fault. He was sloppy and unsympathetic. I didn't want him to touch me. I felt like a dead girl, watching another strange man plumb my body, humiliate it. Saliva swabs, vaginal swabs, pubic hair combings. My body as evidence, as the crime scene. I wished I could take off my skin and have them seal it away in a plastic bag.

. . .

In only a medical gown, I lay on a bed with privacy curtains in the ER. Uniformed police officers were nearby; I heard their radios. The curtains slid on their metal track and a plainclothes police officer walked in.

"Ms. Thompson," he said. "I'm Detective Mike Gauldin." His was the first compassionate face I saw, despite the fact that he didn't look like he could be much older than I was.

Detective Gauldin explained procedure to me: going to the station to make a statement, the rape crisis counselor who would be available to me. He wanted to know what family he should call, and I told him Paul and my sister Janet. As he talked, I heard another woman crying somewhere in the ER.

"What happened to her?" I asked, nodding in the direction of the sound. He paused for a minute before saying, "She was raped. We think it's the same guy." I began to cry again for her, for both of us. This must have been the first moment I felt the hate. I hated him for what he had done to us. *He's not going to get away with this.*

"Ms. Thompson, did you get a good look at your assailant?" Detective Gauldin asked. "Do you think you'd recognize him if you saw him again?"

In an instant, it was all there: *Shut up or I'll cut you!* His narrow eyes, the pencil-thin mustache, the repulsive lips, the nose so close to my own. His laughter after he asked me if I wanted my ten dollars back and I said, "You stole my money?"

"Yes," I told the detective. "I would."

• • •

Paul drove me to the police station, following the detective. I collapsed in his arms when I saw him, feeling like I never wanted to leave that space. We didn't really talk. He was rumpled and quiet. It was a lot for a twenty-five-year-old guy to take in, especially one like Paul, who had his whole life mapped out.

The last bit of night was leaving the sky, and as the sunrise began to bleach it, I felt filthy and exhausted. The smell of my rapist lingered in my nostrils; it was all over me and I wondered if Paul could smell him, too. Already the gulf between us was so much more than this too-early morning silence. It was a fault line.

I walked into the building; it was the first time I had ever been in a police station. My younger sister, Janet, and her boyfriend, Andrew, were already there. Janet was blond and brown eyed like me, but she was taller and thinner, with a longer face and a wide, easy smile. Andrew was somewhat stocky; his dark Irish looks always reminded me of a young Al Pacino. I clung to Janet for a long time. The police called my parents. They must have reached my father at home in Winston-Salem. My mother was staying at our vacation place, a condo at Grandfather Mountain, because it was near Appalachian State University, where she was taking classes. I remember Janet's speaking to them on the phone, looking at me and telling them, "Yes, *physically,* she's OK." My hand went to the side of my neck where he'd pressed the knife in.

I took the phone, ". . . raped . . . last night . . . police . . ." I heard my voice saying these words, those exacting words cutting through the surreal fog coating everything. "Oh Jennifer," my mother said, sadly. Then, "Do you think it was someone who saw you in your leotard at Spa Lady?" I withdrew deeper into the numb composure that kept me functioning. I told her I had to go, and that I would call soon.

Fatigue gripped every part of me but I fought to remain present, to do what I had to do. I was led into a conference room, where some officers set up a recorder and a small microphone in front of me. Detective Gauldin asked if I wanted Paul to remain in the room while I made my statement. I didn't want Paul to hear any of it, but I knew he would have to know and it was easier to have him there in the room than have to tell him separately.

The record button engaged, and a plastic click set the tape in motion. Facing the microphone, the detectives began to question me. The small wheels spun the tape forward, and I had no choice but to proceed. Detective Gauldin had kind eyes, and I tried to look at them as I relayed the memories of last night that felt carved onto me, like scars I'd never be able to cover. I couldn't bear to look at Paul in the corner.

. . .

It was midmorning when we began the composite sketch; I was grateful for the task and the focus it required. Detective Gauldin brought in an Identi-Kit, a blank canvas on which we would create the face of my rapist. It seemed like the worst kind of irony: All you want to do is forget but instead, in the fluorescent glare of a conference room, they ask you to remember over and over and over.

I looked at pages and pages of eyes, ears, noses, chins. The parts swam in my field of vision, forcing me to linger over the eyes of my rapist, become an expert in the shape of his brows, which were seared in my memory. When Paul and I first met, in those early, bursting moments of infatuation, I would constantly try to recall every part of his face. But I had a vague imprint of him then; I found that I could not isolate his eyes or his smile very well. Only later would I know every scar and crease, the exact shade of his eyes—the features I had grown to love, the features I studied up close in the quiet moments we spent together.

After an hour and a half, we had a face. The mouth wasn't quite right, and the ears stuck out too much, but it was close to the picture in my mind. The police were happy. The other victim wasn't sure she could identify him, so I was determined to do a good job. Around noon, the police department released the composite to the local news.

Detective Gauldin wanted me to return to my apartment with them, so I could let them know if there was anything that looked out of place, something that they might have missed. But before I could even convey the terror I felt about stepping back inside my apartment, uniformed officers interrupted. Something was "incomplete." Detective Gauldin looked frustrated but softened when he spoke to me.

"Did you get a penicillin shot?"

"I don't think so," I told him.

"The morning-after pill?"

I shook my head.

"Ms. Thompson, I've very sorry about this, but we need to get you back to the hospital. We're going to take you to Alamance County Hospital this time, see if they can't do a better job." I could tell he was sorry he had to put me through this.

Another hospital, another rape kit. There was the biology of the crime to deal with; marks that may have been left not just in my shattered psyche and my nightmares, but in the flesh that he'd crawled inside. If there had been any food in me, I would have thrown it all up.

• • •

Afterward, Paul drove me back to the apartment, following the police. We turned down Rosyln Drive and into the parking lot in front of the Brookwood Garden apartments, my building with its pleasant gray brick and blue-shuttered facade coming into view. Did I miss a sign? In the single-story structure before me, divided neatly into apartment units, was there a warning that it wasn't safe? I had lived in another building in this complex only the year before, with a roommate, but I was so excited to be on my own. I wanted to live by myself, to be independent. Now I wondered if I was ever going to be able to be alone again. I knew, at least, that I would never be in *this* apartment alone again.

The scene had already been "processed," Detective Gauldin explained. But coming back in the daylight might give them another chance to collect evidence. I went in, surrounded by police officers. The linens were gone from my bed; Smurfette had been bagged as evidence. Light pushed through the corners of the blinds, still shut as if it was night, and afternoon sun from the unshaded windows filled the rest of the apartment. Gone were the grainy shadows, the treacherous unlit pockets that he had hidden in the night before.

Detective Gauldin asked me to let him know if anything looked disturbed. But as we moved through the rooms, I lingered over everything, saying good-bye. This was no longer my home. Outside my back door, the policemen showed me the broken light, the three jabs into the frame probably made by his knife. It didn't appear to be enough damage to get the door open, the officers explained, pointing out that the door was swollen.

"I've had trouble with it in the past few weeks," I told them. "It's hard to close because it's not fitting snugly into the frame."

It was probably easy for him to pry it open, the officers said.

I showed them the postcards and letters strewn across the coffee table in the den, things that had been neatly piled up, things that he had gone through and read while I'd slept in the next room. Gauldin put them into a bag to dust for latent fingerprints, and then picked something up from the hallway just outside the den.

"Do you recognize this?" he said, holding a small piece of dark foam rubber.

I looked at it. I was—and still am—a meticulous housekeeper. There was no way I would've left something like this on the floor. "No," I told him. "That couldn't have been there before. I would've noticed it."

He nodded and placed it into an evidence bag. Later, this would become key evidence: The prosecutor would hold it up in court and say it had come from the soles of the shoes my attacker had worn.

"Ready to go?" Gauldin said. I nodded, before it hit me. *Where was I going to go?*

• • •

Paul took me to his parents' house, where I finally showered and thought about how I was going to sleep. I was almost embarrassed to face his mother, as if she knew something private about me she wasn't supposed to know. She looked equally displeased with the knowledge, as if it was a secret she wished I had kept. I wondered if being raped by a black man made me a less desirable prospective wife for her son.

My sister and her boyfriend were invited to spend the night, but Paul's mother refused to let Paul and me stay in the same room. "It wouldn't look right," I overheard her whisper.

I wanted to shout, "Don't worry, I have no intention of having sex the night after I've been raped!" but I couldn't marshal the energy. Instead, I was shown to his sister's room, which had three single beds in it. Paul rigged the door with string and pie tins, a Boy Scout heroic booby trap that would alert me if anyone tried to enter while I slept. Janet took the bed next to mine, and I got into bed, letting the mattress underneath me accept all of my weight. I tried to give in to the pull of weariness, the sleep my body so desperately craved. But every time I closed my eyes, I heard things. No sooner would I start to drift when suddenly I would bolt upright, sobbing. Eventually, Janet just got on the narrow bed with me and held me. Suddenly, my younger sister was my protector.

But how would I ever be safe again? Despite a foot pursuit, my attacker had escaped the police and then raped someone again less than an hour later, less than a mile from my apartment. He knew my name, knew things about me.

Somewhere out there in the darkness, he was waiting.

CHAPTER 2

There were three burglaries last night in West Burlington, and two of the burglary victims were sexually assaulted. The police are looking for a black man in his late twenties, approximately six feet tall, slim to medium build, neatly dressed, wearing a navy blue athletic shirt with white stripes on the sleeves, green army fatigue pants, black shoes, and possibly wearing white gloves. Suspect has a pencil-thin mustache. Police released this sketch of the suspect. If you have any information, please contact . . .

—TV Broadcast, July 29, 1984

OVER AND OVER, the local news broadcast the composite image. Radio stations WBAG, WBBB, WPCM, WQRB, and WSML ran similar requests for anyone with information to come forward. A white woman raped in her home in the middle of the night by a black man who had the audacity to outrun the police and the dogs, and then go on to rape another white woman in her home didn't sit very well with the community. A rapist was on the loose.

Paul drove me to Grandfather Mountain, where my mother was staying. It was three hours outside of Burlington, and billed itself as "a sanctuary for the human spirit," which all these years later seems like a bad punch line. The condo was built into the mountain to take advantage of the Blue Ridge views. The first floor had the kitchen, a bathroom, and a bedroom with a queen-size bed. There was a split upper level, with my parents' bedroom on the first split and the last bedroom on the highest level. Sleeping up there felt like sleeping up in the air. I didn't think about it until years later, but for some reason, I was put in the bedroom downstairs, which had a ground-floor window. On the night table, a big flower arrangement, with a "Get well soon" card sticking out of it. I smiled awkwardly. They were my mother's attempt at grace notes, as if I had a bad flu. It was hard to fault her. There was no etiquette guidebook to tell you what to do when someone you love has been raped.

When she asked me if I was all right, scanning me for damage, I answered, "I'm fine." I did this for her benefit, for Paul's, and because I didn't know just how to articulate the emotional squalls I had felt in the two days since my rape. It seemed to be the answer everyone wanted, including me. I guess I thought if I acted like everything was fine, it would be. Despite everything that had happened, my mother's rules about appearances and propriety were no different than Paul's mother's. Paul was not going stay with me in the same room. We weren't married, after all, and how would that look?

· · ·

My mother must have had the dryer going on the other side of the bedroom wall. *Clank . . . Clank . . . Clank.* As something thumped repeatedly against the metal cylinder, turning over and over, I thought of the A/C's rattling in the window on that night, metal on metal, which had prevented me from hearing that someone had broken into my apartment. As I lay in the condo, my heart rate accelerated. He was there. Branches moved outside the window. He'd found me. *Clank.*

Too frightened to cry, I felt like the wind had been knocked out of me. I couldn't get air. I didn't know if I could scream. Fear immobilized me: If I cried for help, he would definitely come in and kill me, but if I didn't scream for Paul or my mother, he would get me anyway. *Clank.*

I don't know how long it took me to make a noise. I tried to get something to come out, but I lay there saying, "Ah, ah"—the sound you make in your dream when you are screaming at the top of your lungs but barely make a whimper. But finally the volume came. I screamed and screamed.

Paul and my mother came running into the room. They found me hunkered down in a ball on the floor with my arms over my head.

"What's the matter?" my mother said.

"There's somebody outside. He's outside the window. I can hear him."

Paul went outside to look and came back, saying he had checked all around but no one was there. My mother put her arms around me and I cried and cried. I felt like a child. She lay on the bed with me, and out of sheer exhaustion, I finally fell asleep.

When I woke up late the next morning, though, she wasn't

there next to me. She knocked on my door from outside the room, to say that the Burlington police were on the phone. They wanted me to come in and look at some photos. Paul and I left almost immediately.

. . .

"Ms. Thompson, Detective Gauldin is going to lay down six photos of black males for you to look at. The suspect may or may not be included in these. Please take your time and study each picture. If you do see the person who hurt you, show us," said Detective Ballard Sullivan, an older officer whose hair—at least what was left of it—was dark red. Like many men who lost their hair, he seemed to make up for it by framing his face with it. A lighter auburn mustache and trim beard gave his otherwise jowly face some definition. I could tell he was the person in charge: Gauldin and the other detective deferred to him. He told me to call him "Sully." Despite the smattering of freckles across his nose that gave him the smudged look of a ten-year-old, Sully wore his authority like a ten-gallon cowboy hat. He did not have a soft side; I figured that compassion, in his line of work, might have worn away over the years.

Detective Gauldin told me not to feel compelled to make an identification, to take as long as I needed. I sat at Sully's desk while Gauldin dealt the mug shots like a pack of cards: three on top, three on the bottom. The detectives stood behind me, and I went through each picture slowly and carefully. The stakes felt awfully high.

My heart raced on adrenaline. I assumed they must have had a suspect. Why would they want me to drive all this way if they didn't? All I had to do was pick him out. And if I failed to do that, would he go free? Would he find me?

Most were easily eliminated, and I narrowed it down to two. When I looked at one photo, the image of the man performing oral sex on me came back so violently I thought I would be sick right there. The memory was too sharp and clear.

"Yeah. This is the one," I said, pointing to the picture. "I think this is the guy."

"You 'think' that's the guy?" asked Sully.

"It's him," I said, clarifying.

"You're sure?" asked Gauldin.

"Positive."

They asked me to date and initial the back of the photo, and then they did, too.

"Did I do OK?" I asked.

Sully and Gauldin looked at each other. Relief washed over me.

"You did great, Ms. Thompson."

It had taken me five minutes.

• • •

When I was young, my family called me "little momma" because I liked taking care of everyone. If my sister or one of my brothers was sick, I'd buy them coloring books and bring them juice. Now I wanted to be taken care of, but everyone was off doing his or her own thing: My brother Joe was away in Europe, which I told myself was why he didn't call. My older brother, Jim, was already married with his own family, living in Winston-Salem. Janet, although she did the best she could, was trying to get through college. The world didn't stop, and so I sleepwalked through my days as they blurred together.

Sadie, my rape crisis counselor, had an office at Elon. I met her that first night in the hospital. She was probably in her forties, with short, curly hair and a dimpled smile. Her soothing, kindly demeanor belied toughness; when she had to be, Sadie was a fighter. She was my advocate, she explained; she would help me through the police protocol and trial, should my case make it there. "I am here for you, whenever you need me," she said. But I wouldn't allow myself to be needy with her. I had a plan. The police were going to get this guy, and he was going to pay. As much as everyone wanted me to forget about it and move on, I would not do that until the man who attacked me was behind bars.

Almost two decades later, right before Sadie retired, she told me that she remembered seeing me walking to school every day before my assault. Once, she had even stopped to offer a ride.

"No, thank you," she said I replied. "I prefer to walk," and continued in the direction I was headed.

"That was you," she recalled. "Always so determined. You didn't want to deviate from your plan."

. . .

Sadie met me at the police station when they brought me in to do a physical lineup. Detective Gauldin thought it would be a good idea for her to be there. It was August 8, 1984, eleven days after my assault. He called me the day before to say the lineup was set for 2:00 P.M. the next day, and that Sully, the bearded detective I had met during the photo identification, would drive me to and from the station.

I sat in a chair in the detective's office with Sadie. Detective Gauldin came in. "How are you holding up?" he asked gently.

"I'm fine," I said. I didn't want him to see me as weak or unfocused, to be worried that I couldn't do this.

"Here's how it's going to work: You're going to be shown seven black males of similar appearance. They will be standing in a line, holding a card with a number. Each of them will step forward, turn completely around to the right, say something, and step back. If after viewing all seven you are able to say that one of them was the person who raped you, write his number on the piece of blank paper you are going to be given and hand it to me. If you don't see the man who raped you, leave the paper blank and hand it to me. If you're not sure, leave the paper blank and hand it to me. If after seeing all seven you want any of the men to repeat the procedure, just ask me. Don't feel compelled to make an identification. Make sense?"

I nodded.

"All right then, let's go in there."

Sadie and I followed him down a corridor to a basement room. I had only seen stuff like this on TV, where you stood behind a wall with a window in it. Nothing could have prepared me for what I walked into.

I stiffened and tried to suck in air with an audible gasp. There were seven black men lined up against the wall. All that separated them from me was a conference room table. They could see me. Later, I learned that this had been a transitional building—a new Burlington police station was being built near the railroad tracks. But at that moment, I figured that's the way lineups were really done, that TV had gotten it wrong.

"It's OK. I will be right here. Nothing can hurt you," said Gauldin.

Sadie and I stood behind the table. There were maybe six feet between me and the lineup. There were other officers in the room, and some other men I didn't recognize.

Breathe. Breathe, I told myself. I didn't want to pass out, but I was sick with fear. If he was here, now he knew what I looked like in broad daylight. He knew my name. If he was here, I couldn't screw this up.

Starting with the man holding a card that read "1," each stepped forward, closer to the table, turned to the side, then back to the front, and spoke.

"Shut up or I'll cut you! Hey, baby, how ya doing? Your man's over in Germany. It's been a long time."

The words hit me like a punch to the stomach. Hearing what that man had uttered to me, his face right above mine. I had to make my mind split, the way it had that night. I didn't want to make eye contact with any of them, despite trying to look at each of them closely. I concentrated on my job—to find him if he was here—even though my mind vividly replayed scenes as each man repeated the lines.

Number four began his turn. He had on a light yellow shirt and jeans. A shudder of recognition went through me. Was this him?

Number five went, next. When he said, "Shut up or I'll kill you!" I froze. He and number four looked so much alike, so much like my attacker. Why did he say, "I'll kill you?" I wondered. Was it a trick? He had on a brown and beige mock turtleneck shirt and jeans.

The rest of the men finished. I kept looking at numbers four and five. I turned to Detective Gauldin, "It's between four and five. Can I see them again?" I whispered.

Number four repeated the procedure. His facial features were so close, but his body didn't seem right. My rapist had been lankier.

"Shut up or I'll cut you!"

Number five got it right this time. I looked at his face. He had a light mustache; his eyes looked cold. His body was long and lean. He knew to wear brown, I thought, because he knew he had been wearing dark blue the night of my assault. And he knew to wear his hair differently.

It was him. There was no doubt in my mind.

I knew it. If I didn't get him, he was going to come after me. The terror simply took my breath away. He was standing right in front of me, and if the police didn't lock him up, surely he would walk out of there, find me, and finish the job. The next time, I was certain, I would not get away. He would kill me.

I wrote "5" on the piece of paper in front of me, and slid it over to Detective Gauldin. He nodded, and showed it to a few other men in the room. Then they led me back out, into the hallway.

As always, I wanted to know how I had done.

"We thought that might be the guy," said Gauldin. "It's the same person you picked from the photos."

My knees nearly gave out from under me. *We got him.* Sadie squeezed my hand, proud of me. There were so many others who never even got this far, she told me. So many who would never tell anyone what had happened to them, much less seek prosecution.

• • •

With Joe off in Europe, my family worked it out so I could stay at his place in Chapel Hill, since there was no way I was going back to Brookwood Gardens. Being in Chapel Hill meant I would be closer to Paul, who would be returning to graduate school there after the summer at home with his parents. He and Janet and Andrew packed up my stuff and moved me.

I resumed my classes at Elon, driving to Burlington every day, trying to keep myself occupied. If I was busy, I could fake it OK. But if I was by myself, the events of that night would constantly run through my head. My move to Chapel Hill put a tremendous burden on Paul. I now needed him desperately. Looking back, I know I must have suffocated him. Chapel Hill had been his refuge, and I invaded it. He couldn't get back to his schoolwork or his friends without my resentment. He was twenty-five years old, and the next two years of business school would be hard to get through if he was constantly tending to me.

One evening, we were at his apartment. He had some friends over and they were watching *Risky Business*. It suddenly became very threatening—the sexual content of the movie, the way women were portrayed. It felt personal.

I went into the kitchen with Paul as he got more beers. "Can you tell them to turn it off?" I asked him. "I just—I can't watch it."

He kissed the top of my head and walked back out into the den.

"Guys, can you turn that off? It's making Jennifer uncomfortable."

I listened from the kitchen.

"She's just gonna have to get over it, man."

The movie stayed on, and I went into Paul's bedroom alone.

Janet made a promise to my parents that she would be there

for me, and she was. But she had her classes at Elon and her boyfriend, and I urged her to return to them. I'm fine, I told her. After all, people told me all the time that I was lucky. "Did he beat you?" they asked. "Cut you?" When I shook my head no, they shrugged. They were sorry it happened to me, but it just didn't seem like that big a deal, because it was just sex.

Janet was bigger than me—a whole four inches taller—so even though she was my younger sister, she acted as if she were the older one. She always had this tough act about her.

Several months before, Janet and I had taken a walk near my apartment, winding up near a lake on campus populated by ducks. We had been walking for maybe an hour or so, and the conversation wandered from one thing to another.

"What would you do if you were ever attacked?" she'd asked.

"I dunno. I guess I'd probably try to stay calm, you know, talk my way out," I'd told her.

"Not me! I'd punch him, hit him. I'd kick my way out," she'd replied, doing one of the moves from her kick-boxing class. "They'd be sorry they messed with me."

"OK, Supergirl," I'd said, laughing.

• • •

A few weeks following the physical lineup, Paul and I went to Swenson's Ice Cream in an attempt at normalcy. To outsiders, we must have looked like a typical couple, escaping the August heat and indulging our sweet tooth. I ordered cookies and cream, which had always been my favorite. While I picked at the scoop, I tried to remember what the simple pleasure of my favorite flavor was, before all this. I saw a storm cross Paul's face, his brows knitting together, trying to work something out. "What?" I asked.

"I can't understand why," he said, struggling. "Why didn't you fight back?"

The ice cream went sour in my mouth. I put my spoon down, feeling tears pool in my eyes.

"I told you. I did what I thought I had to do to survive. He was bigger than me. He had a knife. At my throat." I was shocked that I had to defend myself to the one person I felt closest to.

He was silent for a few minutes. I could see that the answer hadn't quite settled him. Doubt still expanded in his gut, pushing him to continue.

"Then I need to ask you," he said, more quietly now, without looking at me. "Did you like it?"

The relationship ended then, although we would continue to pretend it hadn't for several more months. Something essential had been lost in the interrogation room the day of my assault, as Paul sat there for my support but instead came to the conclusion that I didn't fight *hard enough* and that somehow being raped at knifepoint may have actually been enjoyable.

How can anyone say, in those moments, what "enough" is? Just two weeks after my attack, the body of Deborah Sykes was found in Winston-Salem, my hometown. She was four years older than me, and she was raped, sodomized, and stabbed sixteen times one morning on her way to work. One wound plunged five inches into the left ventricle of her heart, and her killer left her to bleed to death in a field across from the fire station. If I had fought differently, if I had fought more, would I have died in my bed that night? If Deborah Sykes had fought less, or differently, would she have crawled out of the grass alive, to take her place among those of us who survive, the walking dead?

That day in Swenson's was not the first or last time I wished my rapist had cut my face or broken my nose or left some kind of physical proof so I could look at someone and say, "Don't you see this? I'm in pain."

CHAPTER 3

HIS NAME was Ronald Cotton.

I loathed the way it sounded. "Cotton" made me think of the too-small white knit gloves he had worn, the fabric nearly suffocating me as he pressed his hand down on my mouth.

"He's going to be sorry he messed with you," Sadie said.

Yes, I thought, *that bastard is going to be very sorry.*

• • •

I wanted to know more. I always needed more information. The monster had a name, but did he have a family? Was I the first woman he had done this to? In some fragment, some piece of evidence the police found, maybe I could begin to understand. I had no badge of pain I could wear to show everyone the lingering effects of being within inches of my life that night, certain I would die at the hands of Ronald Cotton if I hadn't been able to escape.

Instead, I built a facade of control, scaffolding it with every bit of information given to me.

Sully told me Ronald Cotton was from the area, had grown up in the projects around Burlington and Glen Raven with five sisters and two brothers, and that he had four more sisters and two brothers—half siblings, I think—scattered throughout the county. He worked at Somer's Seafood, which was close to my Brookwood Gardens apartment. One of the managers had called when he saw the composite. Said the drawing looked an awful lot like a busboy who worked there. The police also told me a witness had seen Ronald Cotton riding his bicycle near Front Street, wearing white gloves. He had gotten out of prison in February for breaking and entering, and when he was sixteen years old, he'd served eighteen months for breaking and entering with intent to commit rape.

"She was white, too. Only fourteen," sneered Sully. He told me Ronald Cotton liked white women.

A scumbag, they called him. A real scumbag.

. . .

The manager of Brookwood Gardens apartments was an older man, grandfatherly. He used to collect the mail I still got at my old apartment and drop it off for me. One day before heading off to classes, I was going through my bills. I opened one without noticing the return address first.

"Oh my God," I remembered saying aloud.

It was a bill from Memorial Hospital, which claimed I owed about five hundred dollars for the pleasure of my ER visit, the incomplete rape kit and exam. I crumpled and threw it into my school bag. When I showed the bill to Sadie, I said, "Do I really have to pay for this?"

She looked at it in disbelief, furious on my behalf.

"Absolutely not. You should have never even seen this. The State always pays. I'll make sure it's dealt with," she said, adding it to a tray of papers on her desk.

. . .

The Burlington district attorney's office called me to tell me Ronald Cotton would have a probable cause hearing on August 28. I had no idea what a probable cause hearing was. Were they going to set bail and then he was going to be out in a month? Was he going to come find me? Why did we need a preliminary hearing? To me it was simple: I had been raped, the police caught the guy, and I picked him out of a lineup. Shouldn't he be tried and thrown into jail as soon as possible? And if there was a death penalty, I wanted Ronald Cotton to get it. I would pull the switch if they let me.

As I struggled to keep up with my studies, I got a crash course in the criminal justice system. I drove down to Graham, which was about ten minutes away from Burlington. Graham, they told me, was the county seat, so if the charges were deemed serious enough at probable cause, the case would be tried in Alamance County Superior Court. Graham was a sleepy little place—the whole downtown seemed to revolve around the courthouse, quite literally. East Main Street and its single-screen cinema and discount shops led directly to it, sitting in the middle of a traffic circle. You could only drive one way around it, so I would turn right and pass the law offices and store fronts advertising for bail bonds before heading down Elm Street, where the district attorney's offices were.

The assistant district attorney, James Roberson, told me to call him Jim. As soon as I saw him, I was glad he was on my side. Between his elegant blue suit and thick head of hair, he reminded me of John F. Kennedy, distinguished and articulate.

He explained that probable cause was "procedure" to ensure the prosecution had a case against Ronald Cotton.

"Don't worry about that," Jim said, immediately reading the fear on my face. "We've got an excellent case. But I think you know the second victim didn't pick Ronald Cotton at the lineup, so we're not going to try her case. But we can get him on yours, if you take the stand and tell the judge what happened to you. Do you think you can do that?"

Ironic. My rape was an unmentionable in my family, with my friends. No one wanted to talk about it. Yet I would have to describe it over and over again to complete strangers: the police, the judges, the jury. The details. It felt humiliating and disgusting, but I knew what he was saying. He needed me to nail Cotton. The other victim, Jim said, was fragile. She cried easily and simply wouldn't be able to help. I would make sure Ronald Cotton paid for what he did to us. That was the goal now. He didn't catch me the night I ran; he wasn't able to kill me and shut me up forever, although I was sure he sat in his jail cell every night wishing he had.

"I'm going to be honest with you, Jennifer," Jim continued. "It's going to be tough on you. They will go through everything— what you wore that night, the last time you had sexual intercourse and with whom . . ."

Mike Gauldin had told me the same thing. But it never felt like a choice to me. If I didn't testify, Ronald Cotton would go free. In the space of a half hour, this man had destroyed my life. I couldn't imagine not going all the way through with it. I knew exactly who had hurt me, and if I didn't make sure Ronald Cotton went down, he would certainly go on to rape other women. I told Jim I could do it.

"Good. We're going to get him, Ms. Thompson. He's not going to hurt anyone again."

Then Jim asked me to tell him exactly what happened that night. I nodded, took a deep breath, and focused, mustering a false bravado to match his confidence in me.

When I finished, I could tell I passed. Despite the biomechanics exam crumpled in my bag, marked with the first C I ever got, I was getting an A with flying colors in being a witness. I knew it was the most important test I would ever have.

• • •

The probable cause hearing was the first time I entered a courthouse, which was just a block from the DA's office. It was not the big courthouse I passed on the drive in from Burlington, but a smaller-looking building that could just as easily have been a post office. It was clean and contemporary inside, as if the clinical building might banish the ugly, messy realities of crime.

In the row behind us sat a woman who looked maybe fortysomething. I don't remember who introduced us, maybe it was Detective Lowe, who had worked her case. Her name was Mary Reynolds, and she was the woman who had been raped an hour after me. She introduced me to her daughter, who I thought must be about my age. Mary was probably as old as my mother. We were so different, at least on the surface. *Why us?* I wondered. Were we random victims? Planned?

Over the course of the investigation, I learned that Ronald Cotton slapped and bit Mary during her assault; she'd screamed and fought. He'd left bruises, marks. While he raped her, he had shone a flashlight directly into her face. I wondered if he did that because he knew I had seen him. He'd eventually gotten off her and run when he heard sirens. Mary and I would never talk about any of it. Or really talk much at all. All we had in common, after all, was something neither one of us wanted any part of.

When Jim said, "The State calls Jennifer Eileen Thompson," I stood up with shaking knees and walked by the table that Ronald Cotton sat at with his attorneys. It was the closest I had been to him since the day of the lineup. I sat in the witness box, looking down at the people lining the rows. Detectives Gauldin and Lowe were there. And Mary. They were counting on me. My words had saved me that night, I was sure of it. Now I needed them to get him.

There weren't many other people in the court that day. I don't really remember what I said, but Jim looked pleased when I finished. I slid back into the pew feeling emboldened. The playing field was different in the bright lights of the courtroom. My rapist's knife didn't give him any power in here. Jim continued arguing things on behalf on the State, technical things that I couldn't always follow, but he must have done a great job convincing the judge, because he announced that he was increasing the bond on each individual charge: first-degree rape, first-degree breaking and entering, and first-degree sexual offense. Instead of being held on

$150,000, the bond was now $450,000. Ronald Cotton would not get out before the trial.

. . .

In October, my brother Joe returned from Germany after a six-month-long backpacking adventure through Europe. Just a year younger than me, he had always possessed a frantic energy, an excitement about the possibilities of the world that I would have understood only three months before. Now I felt stuck, frozen.

We stood in his kitchen and he hugged me. "I'm so sorry about what happened to you. You can stay for another day or so, but . . ." he said, somewhat apologetically; he wanted his place in Chapel Hill back. It was as close as we would ever come to talking about what had happened to me. The message in the ellipsis, the omission, was clear. *It's time for you to move on.*

Life just whirled on without me. Even if I could have forgotten about my rape, packed it up like the things from my old apartment now collecting dust in storage, I still had the trial coming up, which would have forced me to remember it anyway. And the trial meant I was going to be spending a lot of time in Burlington.

I found an apartment in a complex called Trail's End, which was much farther from campus than my Brookwood Gardens place had been. Instead of walking, I drove to school every day, at least on the days when I made it to class.

Uncertain about whether I'd be able to live alone, I took a two-bedroom, in case I wanted to get a roommate. This time, the apartment was a two-story townhouse, with its bedrooms on the second floor. Most nights I found myself locking the doors and the windows downstairs, then double-checking them. When I went upstairs, I would close and lock my bedroom door and move a piece of furniture in front of it. I had a phone in the bedroom, within arm's reach from the bed. But nothing made me feel safe.

I had done everything right, all the things girls are told growing up: Don't go out jogging by yourself at night. Lock the doors in your car. Avoid dark alleys. I knew them all. I had done none of these things to put myself in danger. I had been asleep in my bed, my doors locked, I'd been alone. I hadn't been drinking. I'd done everything right and still found myself at the end of a knife blade. So what did that say about how vulnerable I was?

Many nights, I could hear someone coming up the stairs. Ronald Cotton might be in prison awaiting trial, but I was positive someone was there. Outside my bedroom door.

"Burlington Police," the dispatcher answered.

"This is Jennifer Thompson. There's someone in my apartment," I whispered.

"Someone has broken into your apartment?"

"Yes, someone's here. Please help me!"

"Ma'am, where are you located?"

"34 Sherry Drive, the Trail's End apartments."

"Ms. Thompson, we're sending a unit out."

At least once a week all the way up to when the trial ended, I'd put in calls to the Burlington Police Department. Looking back now, I'm sure Detective Gauldin must have asked the force, which wasn't all that big, to handle it whenever I called. Uniformed officers would arrive. They'd check my closets and look under the kitchen sink, open the bathroom drawers. It was crazy, I knew. But they never made me feel stupid. They'd just search my apartment until I felt certain that no one was hiding there, and then they'd leave. I would cry myself to sleep, or, if I couldn't sleep, I'd drink whatever alcohol I could find around the house.

. . .

I don't really know what I would have done without Mike Gauldin and Sadie. As I was preparing for the trial, Mike and I went for coffee a few times.

"Did you always want to be a cop?" I asked him once.

"Well, at first I was going to school for business, but I met a guy who used to be a cop, he told stories all the time about being a cop in Chicago. And that was it, there was no going back. I knew that was what I wanted to do. I wanted to help people."

I learned that he had grown up in a tiny farm town called Pelham and married his high school sweetheart. He was like a moviestar version of a cop: heroic, wildly good looking— the Marlboro Man who'd make you safe.

. . .

When Paul was with me, I would feel safer. I didn't need to call the police then. But as the semester went on, Paul stayed in Chapel Hill during the week. On weekends, he would come into Burlington to see me, his family, and the tight-knit circle of friends he had known since kindergarten. Before he could spend time with me, he always needed to finish a long list of chores his mother laid out for him to do. We fought a lot. Especially on the nights when he would want to return to Chapel Hill.

"Please stay," I'd beg him. "Don't go yet."

"I can't be with you twenty-four hours a day!" he exclaimed, exasperated. "I have to get back to school, to my apartment, my life!"

I'm not sure who was more demanding, me or his mother. It was hard to cut him any slack when I felt so abandoned and alone.

Even worse, I now hated his beloved hometown of Burlington. Coming to Elon College seemed like one of the worst decisions I had made. We argued constantly over where we would live once we got married, since there was no way I would stay in Burlington.

"Why can't we live in Greensboro? It's only half an hour away!" I said, near tears.

"How many times do I have to tell you? The family business is here. I'm going to work with my father."

"But you can drive in from Greensboro—"

"I want to live *here*. This is where I belong."

"Well, I can't. I can't live my life here."

"So where does that leave us?"

• • •

If I wasn't so close to graduating, I would have transferred to another school. But I had invested too much in my education, and I'd be damned if Ronald Cotton, who had taken so much from me already, was going to take that away from me.

But for a hometown-proud guy like Paul, my feelings about Burlington widened the gulf growing between us. It was as if I was stranded on a rickety rope bridge suspended between where I was and the future I once saw for myself. I was fighting like hell to get across, but the closer I got, the more elusive the other side grew. All I could do was cling more tightly to Paul as if, were he and I in the same physical place, perhaps we'd still have a chance to get to the other side of all of this.

Even if Paul had been able to be there twenty-four hours a day, seven days a week, I don't know if it would have been enough. No one could be there in my mind, in the moments that flashed across my brain when I heard a strange noise or could not fall asleep. No one would ever really know what those thirty minutes in the dark had been like, except of course, for Ronald Cotton.

• • •

Paul's friends were goodtime guys who had grown up in the tonier sections of Burlington. Their parents—doctors and lawyers and judges—were upstanding, church-going citizens, members of the country club. These sons of Burlington partied with arrogance and impunity, knowing they would get away with mostly everything they did, and even if they did get into some trouble, it was nothing money couldn't get them out of. After Paul finished school, he would come home and be looked up to in the community, just like his father.

One evening, we went to his friend Mark's party. Mark's parents were out of town, and throngs of people were moving around the Colonial-style house. Word must've spread about this party, because most of the people looked unfamiliar, a mix of Burlington townies and students from Elon. I waited in the bathroom line behind two girls who must have been students at Elon. I leaned against the wall, listening:

"They caught that guy—"

"The one who raped those women?"

"Yeah. One of them went to Elon!"

"I heard that! Thank God! It freaked me out thinking he was

out there, walking around. I stopped working late in the campus library."

"Hey, do you know who it was?

"The guy? Some ex-con or something."

"No—the girl. The one who went here?"

"A guy from my boyfriend's frat knows. I think he said he was pretty sure it was a girl from his business class. She dropped out, I think."

"I would've, too!"

When the bathroom door burst open and a guy stumbled out, they giggled and went in together. I was livid. It was so easy for everyone else to know what I should or shouldn't have done. If I dropped out, what would I have to do but think about my rape twenty-four hours a day? Plus if I was going to be a witness in this case, I had to stay in this stupid town. I needed to graduate as soon as possible so I could leave forever.

I found Paul in the living room with a bunch of his buddies, snorting cocaine off the mirrored coffee table. His friend Johnny, wiping his nose, looked up at me and offered me a tightly wound-up dollar bill.

"Want some?" he said. "It makes you happy."

I would have done anything to make myself happy.

I wanted desperately to still fit into Paul's life. I did not want to be Jennifer, Paul's trauma victim girlfriend. I grabbed the bill and bent over the table, observing my reflection. What would the DA think about his star witness now? Did Paul still see me as his future wife? I scarcely recognized myself.

The cocaine didn't make me happy. But it made me not care

for a while that I wasn't happy. For once, I didn't care that I was miserable. And that was a big improvement.

. . .

Ronald Cotton pleaded not guilty to all charges at the arraignment early in November. Jim told me that meant trial by jury, and the trial would begin in January. During finals week in December, I struggled to concentrate, eager to get through my exams and go home. I had never really hung around much with people from the campus, because I lived off-campus and dated a local guy. So at school, no one had any idea that while they were off skiing during the winter break, I would be stuck in Burlington attending my rape trial.

I drove back to Winston-Salem for Christmas. The house we lived in was the very same one in which my mother had grown up. Her father had founded the oil company my father worked at for more than twenty-five years. We'd moved into my grandparents' home after it had caught fire with my grandmother inside while my grandfather was out tending his roses. Although my grandmother was not injured, it was enough to scare everyone. On the large lot, my grandparents built a smaller house for themselves and my parents moved us into the original house next door. Built in the early fifties, it was big enough that my brothers and sister and I could each have our own room, essential once we became teenagers. It had a bomb shelter in the basement, and a cabana-style patio in the back with a pool table. In warm months, this was where my siblings and I would hang out.

Over the holidays, Joe and his trip to Europe took center stage. Everyone wanted to hear about his adventures. Not a word was mentioned about the upcoming trial. I wasn't sure if my family avoided it because they thought it would make me uncomfortable or because it would make them too uncomfortable. My mother talked about the college classes she was taking and her selling real estate up at Grandfather Mountain. My sister and I found the irony interesting; our mother's degree would be in communications.

By now, I was used to giving the performance of being fine. But when I went into my room, I noticed some clippings my mother saved for me about Deborah Sykes. What exactly was my mother trying to communicate? To me, they served as a reminder of how confused my life had become. Did my rape not count because I had walked away? Was I "fortunate" to be living this half life, wrapped in a baggy cardigan, opening Christmas presents, but totally numb inside?

· · ·

Just before the trial began, Sadie explained to me that I should not be freaked out if the prosecutor or the defense attorneys chatted amiably outside of the courtroom, during breaks. "They probably play golf together on the weekends," she said. "It's a small town. But in there, they are on different sides. Don't forget that. Jim and Mike are on your side."

I had hoped to be in the courtroom every single day, although Jim explained that the defense might do something called a "motion for sequestration" to keep me out on the days I wasn't testifying.

"They want to keep the jury from seeing you too much and sympathizing with you. And that's exactly why I want you in there. Those men and women will look at you constantly throughout the trial as their sister, their daughter, their friend he could have hurt. I know you're going to do a terrific job, Jennifer."

My parents told me they would come when they could. "Your father's got a lot of business meetings," my mother said on the phone. "And you know I've got my classes . . ."

CHAPTER 4

ALAMANCE COUNTY SUPERIOR COURT was a massive marble building, lined by six columns in the front and six in the back. It was by far the most ornate building I had seen in Graham, or Burlington, for that matter. My "sensible" two-inch pumps clacked on the tile floor as we walked in on a morning as gray and cold as stone on January 7, 1985. The courtroom, itself, seemed cavernous, intimidating. It was very different from the courtroom where the probable cause hearing had taken place. The ceilings soared maybe twenty feet above me, and portraits of former judges lined the wood-paneled walls. The judge sat up high on his bench, looking down at all of us. I remember thinking, for a person who was presiding over matters of law and order, he looked rather formless under his robe. Just a plump, balding head with glasses.

The motion for sequestration had been denied, so I could sit in the courtroom for all the proceedings. I wanted to be there even for the jury selection, although my parents would not come until the actual trial began. The lawyers began to explain the process of jury selection from the group of people who had been called in. They debated which individuals they wanted or didn't want and why. Talk about a small town. One woman said she recognized me as an instructor from Spa Lady. Another man raised his hand and said he knew Jim Roberson; another knew the defense attorney, Phillip Moseley; and yet another said he knew Dan Monroe, a guy who was working with Moseley. There wasn't much for me to do but watch, and I was on the edge of the bench, listening intently. The lawyers seemed to spar as if it was a sport, but this was my life. It was no game to me.

After twelve jurors and two alternates were selected, the judge told us all to go home and get a good night's sleep. The trial would be in session at 9:00 A.M. the next morning.

• • •

I barely got any sleep, and finally got out of bed at five thirty in the morning. I made an enormous pot of coffee, which was probably not the best thing for my already nervous stomach. I laid out my outfit and stared at it: a navy blazer and tailored skirt, something I'd wear to a job interview if I were going to work in a bank. I thought it made me look serious, professional, and competent. And the way I looked would be just as important as what I said, Jim said. He told me the trial would be an enormous emotional burden. Not only would I have to tell everyone in the court exactly what had happened to me, in explicit detail, but also the defense would bring up anything it could to make me look unstable and promiscuous. "It's classic blame-the-victim strategy," Jim said. "Don't let it unnerve you." While I watched the sun rise in Burlington, I coached myself. I could do this. What kind of people would judge a woman who had been asleep in her bed when she was attacked?

My parents arrived and met us in a small room near the courtroom. My mother was a tiny blonde, too, with such enormous round brown eyes that sometimes my brothers jokingly called her Marty Feldman, for the comedian with the bulging eyes in their favorite movie *Young Frankenstein,* but she was always very pretty. She had on an elegant dress suit, and my father wore a suit that seemed to match his slate-colored eyes. My father's face was kind, but his eyes were pinched in the outer corners, turning down, giving the overall effect of sadness. When I hugged my mother, I noticed when she pulled away that she glanced at the hem of my skirt. I had steeled myself for a ruthless cross-examination by the defense attorneys, but not from my mother. I was instantly self-conscious about wearing a skirt with a hem above the knee.

Jim came in with his briefcase. He told me I would spend most of my time in this room during breaks and recess. I was not to go out in the hallways alone. "It's for your own protection," he said. "You don't want any run-ins with Cotton's family."

"Definitely not," I said, alarmed at the prospect.

"Ready?" he said. I nodded and began to follow him into the courtroom, tugging at the hem of my skirt.

I sat in the row directly behind the prosecution table, my parents and Paul on either side of me. The defense attorney looked over from the defense table and immediately I looked away, but nonetheless, he made his way over.

"Ms. Thompson, I'm Phil Moseley. I just want you to know I'm very sorry for what happened to you." Tall and lanky, with thick blond hair and bushy eyebrows, Phil Moseley had a complexion so pale that his face reddened easily. His cheeks flushed slightly as he held his hand out politely, and I extended mine limply, nodding. How could he defend rapists and face himself in the mirror every day?

I was relieved when he returned to his side. Sadie came in, followed by my sister Janet and her boyfriend Andrew, and they sat down with us. I glanced over at the rows of people behind the defense table filing in. Jesus, was that Cotton's whole family? My own brothers didn't even show up.

Hopped up on caffeine already, a jolt went through me when they brought Ronald Cotton in. If I was this scared, I hoped he was petrified.

I knew that on some level, I had to perform. I didn't think about it consciously but I knew. If I went up there and told my story and never flinched, it would be perceived as one thing, and if I went up there and just cried and couldn't get a sentence out, it would be another thing. The jury would think I was so highly emotional, how could I possibly have gotten a good look at my assailant? Ronald Cotton might have been the one on trial, but I would be judged, too.

When the judge repeatedly referred to me as "Jennifer Elaine Thompson" instead of "Jennifer Eileen Thompson," it didn't bother me. He could have called me anything. "Jennifer Eileen Thompson" didn't really exist anymore.

. . .

"The State calls Ms. Jennifer Eileen Thompson."

My hands were freezing cold and my teeth were chattering. All the blood rushed to my pounding heart as adrenaline, lack of sleep, and caffeine caught up with me. I clenched my jaw and stood. Getting up onto the witness stand in front of the courtroom, the fourteen jury members sitting along the side, and the judge, was more nerve-racking than I thought. The bailiff asked me to place my hand on the Bible, state my name, and swear to tell the truth. My voice seemed dwarfed by the giant space of the room and the task in front of me.

Almost immediately, the judge said, "You appear to have a soft voice. That means you have to speak up a little louder than you would in a normal conversation so your voice will carry to all the jurors, as well as to other folks involved in the trial of this case."

Jim asked the bailiff to check to see if both microphones were working. Embarrassed, I castigated myself. *Don't screw this up.* I couldn't let them down now. *Focus. Breathe. Your life depends on this.*

I shook off my fear and glanced at Jim. He nodded. I looked at the jurors and told them in a loud, clear voice how I woke up on July 29 to find a man straddling my waist and threatening to kill me. I told them he raped me.

"Let me step back to when he performed oral sex on you. Particularly, did he place his lips on your vagina?" asked Jim. My face flared with humiliation to have to say these things in a room full of strangers. The few people I wanted to talk about my rape with didn't want to hear much about it. Did I really have to explain what oral sex was?

Jim pressed on, "If you would describe for the court what he did with regard to oral sex?"

I could see my father in his business suit, blinking back the tears. Something about having to listen to the graphic description of a rapist's mouth on his little girl seemed to hit him. His whole face purpled brightly trying to contain himself. I thought he was going to hemorrhage.

"He—he used his—he used his—his—he used his lips and he used his tongue," I said, sobbing. Then I looked at Jim. "Do I have to say it?"

The judge ordered a break.

They whisked me off into the private room, and my father came in. He took my hand and squeezed it, unable to express the emotion corralled in his face.

· · ·

"Jennifer, do you see the man in the courtroom today who was in your apartment on the early morning hours of July 29, who had sexual intercourse with you, oral sex with you, and broke into your apartment?"

"Yes," I answered, glaring at Ronald Cotton, who sat there expressionless, as if he didn't care at all what had been done to me.

"Would you point to him?"

I raised my index finger and pointed directly to him, wishing I had had a gun instead and could get a clear shot at him, so I'd never have to see that face again.

"Let the record show that she has pointed to the defendant. Jennifer, are you absolutely sure that Ronald Junior Cotton is the man?"

How could I ever forget? Didn't they know his terrible face would stay in my mind forever?

"Yes," I said.

. . .

Under cross-examination, Moseley made me clarify for the court that all I was wearing that night was underwear, but then he insisted on calling them "panties" in each subsequent question. I caught on to his game. He wanted to know if I pulled down the blinds enough so that no one saw me in my "panties." Every time he said the word, he loaded it as if only someone who would be asking for rape would wear them.

Somewhere in his questioning, he got me to admit that I had a fear of waking up to find someone in my room, watching me while I slept. He pounced on that. "If you have a fear of someone standing over your bed watching you, would it not seem more appropriate for you to go to bed with some kind of nightgown on or something, Ms. Thompson?"

Son of a bitch, I thought, glaring at him. "I don't know that it makes any difference what I would have worn that night. I think if I had had on blue jeans and a sweatshirt, that would not have made any difference in the world, and if I walk outside my bedroom stark naked, that doesn't give anybody the right to—to take what's not theirs."

He tried to recover quickly: "That's your answer?"

"That's my answer."

Then he asked me if I received counseling for my fears. I couldn't believe it. I remarked that when I was young I had a fear of octopuses, but I didn't get counseling for that. Every attempt Moseley made to outwit me, to make me look crazy or promiscuous, only made me more determined. His next tactic was to get me to admit I was a light sleeper. If I was such a light sleeper, he argued, how could I have slept through someone's breaking in, rummaging through my things, and then crawling alongside my bed?

I couldn't say what I really wanted to—which was, what the hell did that have to do with being raped? Instead, I merely explained the crappy old air conditioner made so much noise that I had to shut it off just to watch TV. *Just try to trip me up,* I thought. *You're not going to.*

. . .

Over the next few days, the defense trotted out Ronald Cotton's family as his alibi witnesses. The alibi he had given to the police about being out at a club wasn't true. The defense explained that Ronald had gotten his days mixed up, that was all. *More like, told a pack of lies,* I thought. He was a criminal. What did they expect?

One by one, members of his family took the stand and said he had been at home, asleep on the couch. It was so pathetic, I thought, as if they had all been given a script to memorize. Each one of them said the same thing, almost verbatim: "Well, I remember watching TV, and going into the kitchen and Ron was sleeping on the couch in a light shirt and blue jeans." Gee, you think Phil Moseley rehearsed that with them? I hated Phil Moseley. How could anyone possibly want to be a defense attorney and write this stuff so a rapist could go free and walk the earth?

During one of the breaks, I told the bailiff in the room I needed to use the bathroom. No one was available to escort me, and I told him I was fine. As I stood in front of the sink, washing my hands, the door opened. Out of the corner of my eye, two women walked in who I figured were related to Ronald Cotton because they immediately went quiet. I washed my hands continuously until they went into the stalls, careful not to look up or make eye contact. They were horrible people, I thought, liars, all of them. What kind of evil ran through their veins?

· · ·

On the days that I didn't testify, I looked around at the people on the other side. Consistently, Ronald Cotton must have had three times more people there than I did.

During the closing arguments, the defense asked, "Where is the physical evidence?"

Dan Monroe, one of the defense attorneys, paced in front of the jurors and said, "We don't have any physical evidence, none whatsoever, no fingerprints, no—nothing, no clothing, no nothing that has been linked up to—to this man. Basically, all we've got is Jennifer Thompson on the witness stand saying, 'Yeah, that's him,' and you're asked to be convinced beyond a reasonable doubt, make that quantum leap of faith, that yes, it was him."

Moseley made a point that no "fuzzies"—fibers from my shag rug—were found on Ronald Cotton's shoes. *C'mon,* I thought. He wore gloves. That's why there were no fingerprints. We had an amazing case: There was the piece of rubber they found at my apartment, which was found to be consistent with the shoes they took from Ronald Cotton's apartment; and then there was the witness—the woman who said she had seen him riding his bike right in my neighborhood around four in the morning, in a blue and white shirt. And of course, the fact that Ronald Cotton's alibi to the police was a complete lie.

I expected them to try to make it seem that all this stuff was just "coincidence," but I couldn't believe it when the defense attorney tried to claim this was a case of mistaken identity—that I had been "stressed" after the assault and couldn't properly identify the man who had been lying on top of me. He even had the jury study Ronald Cotton, turning from left to right, pointing out the scars he had that I didn't notice. Earlier in the trial, Moseley had the gall to attempt to bring in some kind of memory expert to testify in front of the jury, although thankfully the judge saw through that and wouldn't allow it. It seemed completely ridiculous. I knew what I'd seen. I would never forget that face. How could I?

One by one, the jurors filed out of the room.

. . .

Jury deliberations took four hours. My parents, Mike Gauldin, Paul, Janet, and I sat in Barrister's Café, just outside the courthouse. The coffee in our mugs had long gone cold before Jim came in to say the jury had reached a verdict. Everyone went quiet, and Jim tried to brace me for the possible outcomes, what the maximum sentence could be. We returned to the courtroom.

I watched the jury walk in, looking at me. These people were entrusted with my life.

When the foreman stood up and said, "Guilty,"—that was the only word I heard—I felt something let go in my body—perhaps the breath I had been holding on to. I don't know if I felt vindication or relief.

I didn't quite follow all the intricacies of the arguments about sentencing. Moseley tried to say that since Ronald Cotton had dropped his knife and didn't hurt me, he should be given a more lenient sentence.

"He put his knife in his pocket and later put the knife outside the room and did inform Ms. Thompson, according to her statement, that he was not going to kill her," said Moseley. *Right there,* I thought, *it proved that Moseley knew his client was guilty.*

The judge took issue with that, saying with welcome sarcasm, "I'm sure when she heard that she placed total reliance in his credibility. You use the word 'hurt,' counselor. That young lady will go to her grave with certain emotional scars as a result of your client's conduct . . . Rape in the common law was a capital offense and it is only the result of *Coker v. Georgia,* in the last decade that the Supreme Court has forbidden, for the moment, capital punishment for the crime of rape, but it is no thanks to your client that she's alive here today. She saved herself by her wits."*

Moseley deferred but tried to keep arguing until the judge cut him off.

"She may not have a scar that goes from the top of her head down to her cheekbone, but she has those emotional scars and they'll be there every bit as long as the physical scars that —few in number though they may be—your client has."

I could have hugged the judge, although he'd probably hold me in contempt of court. Jim argued that Ronald was a serious criminal. "Quite frankly, the State considers Ronald Junior Cotton a menace to the society of North Carolina by reason of his

---

*In *Coker v. Georgia,* 433 U.S. 584, 97 S.Ct. 2861, the U.S. Supreme Court struck down a Georgia law that allowed a person convicted of rape to be "punished by death." The court decided on June 29, 1977, that a death sentence was a disproportionate punishment for the crime of adult rape, in violation of the U.S. Constitution's Eighth Amendment ban on "cruel and unusual punishment."

record in 1980, 1983, and now again." He was worried that even with a life sentence, Cotton could become eligible for parole.

Moseley continued to argue on behalf of Ronald. It was something about whether the sentences should be consecutive or concurrent. I didn't know exactly what the distinction was, but made a note to ask Jim about it later.

And then I remember the judge asking if Ronald Cotton wanted to say anything on his behalf. All he had to say was "No, sir." I thought it was so odd that he didn't say anything. Janet, my nineteen-year-old, rail-thin sister, tried consistently to bore holes into him throughout the trial. She stared at his profile, waiting, watching. We all wanted him to react: to turn and sneer at us, or else look like he was contrite. Something. But he gave us nothing. Blank-faced and silent, he just sat there. It was as if he wasn't even there in the courtroom. They could have done the whole trial without him.

On January 18, 1985, Ronald Cotton was sentenced to life in prison plus fifty years.

• • •

We walked down the steps of the Alamance County Courthouse. Sunlight fell across the square, highlighting a statue of a soldier saluting Main Street. In my quest for any bit of information, I read up on the history of the courthouse and the town of Graham. Right here in the square, a former slave named Wyatt Outlaw had been hanged from a tree on February 26, 1870. Two years before he was killed, he had been appointed a town commissioner. His killers were never arrested. And in 1914, the United Daughters of the Confederacy had raised money for this statue, to honor the Alamance County soldiers who had served in the Confederate army. A box was supposedly buried in the ground under the base of the monument, but no one could say for sure exactly what was in the box. I stopped in the long shadow the soldier threw, wishing I, too, could bury this part of my life in his box.

I walked over to the DA's office with Mike, Jim, my parents, Janet, Andrew, Sadie, and Paul. When we got there, we popped the cork from a bottle of champagne and huddled inside the conference room where I had spent many hours preparing for trial. Jim commended the Burlington Police Department for their thorough investigation.

"I'm confident a dangerous rapist has been removed from the community," said Jim. Then he turned to me. "And we couldn't have done that without you, Jennifer. If only all my witnesses were like you. You made my job very easy."

Paul squeezed my shoulder with his hand. We followed Jim's lead and held up our plastic cups.

"To the justice system," he said.

"The justice system," we toasted.

I sipped the champagne—the bubbles hit the back of my throat where a hard knot had formed. Preposterously, I felt a little like Dorothy in the *Wizard of Oz*, saying good-bye to all the characters who helped me along the way.

I looked at Mike Gauldin, and worked my way over to him. "I don't think I would have gotten through this without you," I said. "Thank you for everything."

He shrugged it off. "Just doing my job." His eyes were still as sympathetic as they were the moment I first saw them, when I was lying in a hospital gown at five o'clock in the morning. "I hope you can move on now." He leaned close and hugged me.

I turned away, my eyes feeling heavy with tears, and found Sadie. As we embraced, she whispered to me, "You know where you can find me if you need me."

Then I maneuvered around the conference table to Jim.

"Good luck with your life," he said.

My sister and Andrew brought me my coat. Paul took my hand.

"You can really put this behind you, now."

"It's finally over."

My head buzzed with the champagne. I nodded, unsure of who was saying what. Not that it mattered—they were all saying the same thing anyway.

We opened the door and a gust of cold air hit us dead on. I shivered again, snuggling close to Paul. "Let's go home," he said.

It was the happiest day I had in the past six months. I had done my job well, and Ronald Cotton would rot in prison.

That night, I lay in my bed and prayed. I prayed for Ronald Cotton to die miserably in jail, alone and afraid. But before he left this earth for hell, I asked that he know the horror of being raped. Sleep came over me easily.

PART 2

Ronald

CHAPTER 5

IT WAS AUGUST 1, 1984, From that day forward, I would always pay attention to the date and the time, memorizing details of what happened and when. My life might just depend on it.

I had gotten home around eleven in the morning. I was living with my mom in the Pate projects on Oak Circle then, and her boyfriend, Joe, was out on the porch when I came home. The police had already been there. He told me they had a search warrant and took some of my stuff, including my shoes, a pair of his shoes, a pair of my sister's shoes, and my flashlight. Inside the apartment, they had left a piece of paper on top of the television, with a description of the crimes and a sketch of the suspect. I ran my hand over my head. I had already heard about it on the news.

"Man, I haven't done anything like that."

"You best get down there and straighten this out," Joe said.

The transmission had long been blown on my car, so my sole transportation was a thirty-inch brown Schwinn that I rode everywhere. Once, I even rode from Burlington all the way to Greensboro, almost twenty-five miles. But that day, I didn't want to ride my bike to the police station. I wanted to face this like a man. And I didn't feel like much of a man arriving by bike.

I asked my neighbor Patricia if I could borrow her car. She told me to make sure I got it back to her by three so she could get to work.

"No problem," I told her, "I'll get things sorted out real quick." But in the back of my mind, I knew that if the police in this town wanted to keep me, they would find a reason. I asked my sister Tudy to come with me in case I needed her to drive Patricia's car back.

On the way there, we picked up Teresa, the girl I had been seeing for a couple of weeks. She came running out to the car, tears streaming down her face.

"Ron, the police were here. They were saying something about some rapes," she said.

"I know. I'm going down to the station now to take care of it," I told her.

"I know you didn't do that," she said. "I'm going with you."

I opened the door and she slid into the back. Tudy sat next to me in front; we drove in silence. We were too afraid to talk, too afraid to make promises about its all being a big mistake and everything working out. That's not the way it is in some Southern towns. At least, not for everybody.

. . .

I trudged up the steps to the police station with Tudy and Teresa in tow. The Burlington Police Department back then was in an old schoolhouse on Fisher Street. The last time I saw the inside of a school was in ninth grade, right before I dropped out because I could help my mother more by washing dishes at the Ramada Inn. This building mostly still looked like an elementary school—it was a two-story brick block—except for the white jail bars on all the bottom windows.

When I got to the door, I could see a plainclothed officer looking out at me from a window on the second story. He stared me down while I tried to figure out why he looked so familiar. Then it hit me: This officer had trailed me before. Riding my bike, I would occasionally notice a Carolina blue Thunderbird following me. Other officers gathered around him, looking down at me.

· · ·

"My name is Ron Cotton. I hear the police're looking for me. I'm here to straighten things out," I said to the sergeant manning the front desk.

A young-looking cop came down to meet me.

"Mr. Cotton, I'm Detective Gauldin."

"I heard y'all are looking for me about a crime that was committed in the community," I said. "I didn't do it."

"Come on in and let's go upstairs and talk about it," he replied. "These are some serious charges."

He searched me and took the lock-blade I had in my right front pocket. It was the knife I always carried—a utility knife, not a weapon. I knew the suspect they were looking for was armed with a knife, but I had nothing to hide. Then he brought me to an interrogation room, just like in the movies.

I've replayed this scene in my head over and over, wondering if there was any way all of this could have come out differently. What if I had worn a different shirt? What if I hadn't gotten my dates mixed up? What if I refused to talk until I had a lawyer present? I would have a lot of time to think about my situation: That was the last time I walked in anywhere as a free man for the next eleven years.

. . .

Detective Gauldin told me I was under arrest. They had warrants out for first-degree burglary, rape, and sexual offense. He and another detective, a skinny, chain-smoking guy named Lowe, advised me of my rights while I read along on a form, initialing each paragraph to show I understood.

"I don't need an attorney, sir. I didn't commit this crime and I want to get it straight." I signed, indicating I was waiving my rights in front of Detective Lowe. I remember thinking, *Why would I need a lawyer when I haven't done anything wrong?* I just wanted to get this over with, so they'd see they'd made a mistake.

"Let's talk about this weekend, Ron," Detective Gauldin said. He was a clean-cut guy, pretty young to be a detective. He ran his hands through his hair a lot like he was real proud of it. "Where were you Saturday night? The evening of July twenty-eighth?"

I was twenty-two years old. I didn't give a lot of thought to my days and nights and what distinguished them from one another. Especially in the summer, where time just seemed to run together.

I went where the party was. I tried to think real hard about the night they were asking about.

I told Gauldin I had been hanging out with my brother Calvin at the boardinghouse on Ireland Street where he was living, and I told the detective we were drinking beer and listening to music. Then I walked over to my friends' place down the road, where we drank some more.

"Do you smoke?" Gauldin interrupted.

"Yeah," I said. *Was that a crime?* He stared at me, waiting for something. "Newports," I told him.

He made some kind of note, twisting his mouth to the side like he was sucking meat out of his teeth while he thought on something. He nodded for me to continue.

"I was there until about 10:20 P.M., then I went back to Calvin's. Then me and my friend went out to the Candlelight Club. I stayed there for a while, then I ran into Janice at the club—another friend of mine—and asked her for a ride home 'cause it was raining."

"About what time was that?"

"Two thirty or three in the morning."

He asked me for the names of the people I had seen at the club, people who could verify I was there, writing down what I was saying. But I noticed he wasn't recording the conversation, so I felt that he could be writing down anything. Then Detective Gauldin asked me to continue with what had happened when I'd left the club.

"Janice gave me the keys and I drove us back to the boardinghouse. She went inside and another friend of ours came out and needed a ride home. Said he'd give me a dollar to drive him. I took him home and went back to the boardinghouse. Janice was waiting outside with our friend Jake, who wanted a ride to his uncle's. He and Janice got in, and we dropped him off, then Janice brought me home."

"To 35 Oak Circle?"

"Yeah. Then me and Janice talked some, and I went in and went to bed."

"What time was that?"

"Around four."

"Did anyone see you come in?"

"No, they were all asleep. I went into the downstairs bedroom and fell asleep on the bed."

. . .

Gauldin made me go through the whole thing again, asking me for details and times. After he finished interrogating me, he opened the door to the hallway and I waited for Lowe. My sister Diane passed by. She must've decided to come by after she stopped by my mom's and heard what was going on. Her face was bunched up with worry, and I hated being responsible for that. But I was glad she had come down, too, even if I couldn't talk to her.

Next, Detective Lowe questioned me. I felt like I was saying the same things over and over. Why weren't they getting it? We took a break at four fifteen. It had been over three hours since I'd been in there. I realized Tudy and my girlfriend must have left a while ago to get the car back. I wished I had hugged each of them before I went upstairs with the detectives, but the police might've taken it as a sign I knew I was guilty, saying good-bye and all.

I was allowed a bathroom break, and an officer watched me as I washed my hands afterward. I pressed them, cold and wet, to my face, trying to calm the panic revving inside me. *Why was this taking so long?*

When I went back into the room, there was an older cop, Detective Sullivan—who everybody called "Sully," standing in there with detectives Gauldin and Lowe. He was the one who had watched me from the window as I crossed the parking lot and started up the steps. Suddenly, it triggered something, and I went back, in my mind, to being about twelve, standing on my grandma's porch on Shepard Street in Burlington. I used to want to be a cop, so when I saw a police officer in action, chasing three black kids from the high school, I thought it was one of most exciting things I'd ever seen. I watched when he caught up with one of them and tackled him to the ground. Then the cop placed the muzzle of his gun on the back of the kid's head and said, "If you breathe too hard, I'll blow your head off."

Sully looked like that cop.

They slammed my black canvas World Cup shoes on the table. I used to wear them to mop up the floors at Somer's Seafood. One time I spilled the dirty water all over them, and I threw them in the washing machine, trying to clean them. The insoles started coming apart, but I didn't care. They were just work shoes.

"You recognize these?" said one of the detectives, holding them up. They were split, cut on the soles all the way from the toe to the heel.

"Yeah, they look like my shoes, but they weren't in that condition," I replied.

They pulled out a plastic bag with a small piece of dark foam.

"You see this piece of material? This came from your shoe, and we found it in Jennifer Thompson's apartment the night you raped her."

"That's because you put it there, then. I don't know any Jennifer. I've never been in her apartment." I said.

Then they held up my red flashlight. "This your flashlight?"

"Yeah."

"You know what kind of batteries are in here?"

"I haven't the slightest idea," I said.

"Well, that's because you stole this from Mary Reynolds and held it in her face when you raped her."

I shook my head no. "I haven't done nothing like that."

"Cotton, Jennifer Thompson already identified you. We know it was you."

"No, no. You got the wrong guy." It felt like the walls were closing in on me. My blood was boiling. The heat spread over me, my muscles tensed with anger. I had an impulse to grab this cop by the collar and slam him against the wall. Maybe then he'd listen to me. But I bit the inside of my cheek, knowing that doing something like that would have made everything worse. They would have just piled on more charges.

"Oh, really?" said Sully. He leaned in real close to me, his nose bent like he smelled shit. He had a real cocky attitude. "What about the time you served in juvie for breaking and entering with intent to rape?" he said, throwing some paper at me. "She was a little white girl, too."

Here it comes, I thought. That old case that wouldn't go away. When I was sixteen, I liked this girl Evie, the younger sister of my friend Jeff. We had messed around some before, but one night I had been out drinking, and I walked into their house and into Evie's bedroom. I slipped into bed with her, thinking we could fool around. I startled her so much she hollered. Her mom caught us, and pointed a shotgun at me.

"I can shoot ya now," she said, "or we can let the police deal with ya."

They charged me with breaking and entering with intent to commit rape. Then the charges were dropped and I thought it was all over.

A year later, I was playing ball in Glen Raven and stopped at the store to buy some drinks afterward. On the way out the store, I passed my mom.

"You 'member that sheriff?" she said. "He's looking for you again on those charges. Said they had spelled Evie's name wrong or something."

It didn't make any sense to me, and I thought maybe my mother had gotten things mixed up. But the next morning she came knocking on my bedroom door.

"Ron! The police're here. Just get it over with."

I jumped up and got dressed.

I walked downstairs and out the door, and the two cops handcuffed me right there on the front steps and put me in the car. My dog King, a black collie, was laying there with his chin on the stoop just looking at me, so sad. Mom said the day I left home, King took off and they never did see him anymore.

They locked me up and a court-appointed attorney came down to see me.

"You're looking at fifty to ninety-five years, Ronald. But I can get you a plea bargain for three years. And if you behave, you'll get out even sooner than that."

I tried to tell him I didn't do anything, but he told me it didn't matter. It was her word against mine, and he scared me up real bad.

I really didn't want to plead guilty, but I didn't think I had much choice. The attorney said it was my best chance. I wouldn't have to go to trial or anything. So I took the plea, and spent eighteen months at Polk Youth Center in Raleigh.

When I got out, I made a couple more stupid mistakes. I got caught breaking and entering, and had just gotten out of prison in February '84. I told myself this was it; it was time for me to grow up and make something of myself. My sisters tried to tell me I wasn't running with the right crowd, and maybe they were right. But that still didn't make me guilty of what these cops were saying I did.

This cop Sully, though, he had already decided I was guilty. I'll never forget him saying, "Saw your girlfriend earlier. You think you're Mr. Big Shot, going around town screwing white women, don't ya? We got your ass."

I knew they were trying to get me to break. But it wasn't going to be like that. I wasn't going to make it easy for them. I looked Sully real steady in the eye. Like a lot of people in town, he didn't like the fact that I had dated white girls. Sometimes walking around, you could feel the racism like a pilot light always on in the back of people's minds, flickering, and just waiting to get turned up.

"I know why y'all are doing what you're doing, but just because I date a white girl doesn't mean I'm going to go out and commit this crime because my girlfriend didn't come over that night."

He glared at me. I clammed up after that. I knew it was a losing battle. Anything I said they were just going to use against me.

Sully opened the door and called in a uniformed officer. "Lock 'im up," he said, pointing to me like I was trash that needed to be put out.

· · ·

The Burlington PD didn't have a holding cell, so they handcuffed me and led me out the door on the side—not the public entrance I had come in before—and put me in a cruiser. I went before the magistrate and was placed under $150,000 bond, and then they took me to the county jail in Graham.

Alamance County Jail was a cesspool and it smelled like it. It was an old, old building that was always having problems with the plumbing, and the odor in August when I arrived was fierce.

After they took all my personal belongings and put them in a brown envelope, they issued me a navy blue jumpsuit, kind of like a mechanic's outfit, and allowed me to make two calls. The first person I rang up was my father, who kept his head about such things. "Hang in there, son. I'll come visit you real soon," he told me. "If they get your bond down to $50,000, I'll see what I can do to get you out of there." Next, I called my mother. She was much more emotional. She came right down with deodorant and some soap, a legal pad, and M&M's—back then, they let family do things like that.

"I didn't do it," I told her.

She cried. She was holding the piece of paper the police had left at her apartment, with a drawing of the suspect and a description of the crimes.

"I just got to wait, they'll see, I wasn't there," I told her. "Lots of people saw me, Mom. I was with Calvin and then we went to the Candlelight Club."

"Ron, what're you talking about? You were right at home. I read the date right here. Your sisters done saw you sleeping on my couch all night."

"What do you mean?" I asked.

"You got the days mixed up. Don't you remember Diane Snipes dropped off Tracy at the house? You opened the door for her. And Joe and your sister Puddin' saw you sleeping on the couch."

My heart started pounding. My mother was right. I had gotten my weekends confused. Which meant the alibi I gave to police was not going to check out at all.

"I'll be back soon as I can, Ron. Make sure you eat in here. You gotta keep your strength up."

She had the same look on her face that she had had years ago, when I was sixteen years old and the cops came for me: a strong black woman utterly powerless when someone else was making all the rules.

That night I dreamed about the old white house in Glen Raven. It had a big woodstove where my mom used to cook a vegetable soup that would last for days. When I got older, I realized she made it because she had so many heads to feed, but we loved it. We couldn't get enough.

The house had three bedrooms, and my sisters Diane and

Tudy, and my brothers Calvin and Terry and I used to run all over the place together. Calvin, whom everybody called "Cotton" was the oldest, followed by Diane. Tudy was just a couple of years younger than me, and she followed me around everywhere the way I followed my brother Calvin. Terry, the youngest, did his best to tag along but I usually told him to get lost, to stay home with my mom. At four years younger than me, he was still the baby and she was very protective. That was lucky for him, because he never had trouble with the law like Calvin and me.

As kids, our favorite place to play was out in the woods. It was shady and cool in the summer, and there was a big pond behind the old Fairstone Fabric Mill where you could swim. There was a rope hanging from a branch of a nearby tree, and you could pull it way back and jump on it like Tarzan, and swing way out over the pond. We'd drop off like stones, plunking down into the dark water.

We'd walk back barefoot, searching for wild grapes called muscadines, our wet shins getting streaked with mud from the creeks. In school when we learned about Thanksgiving, we learned that Alamance County got its name from the local Native American word for that mud, which was kind of bluish. I always remembered that because my grandmother on my father's side was a full-blooded Cherokee, so that meant I had Indian blood myself.

Once when we went swimming behind the mill, I felt a cool breeze threading around my ankles, a current that felt like it was going to pull me under. I swam as hard and as fast as I could to get out of there, and I never did go back in. A lot of people ended up drowning there, and I think it was finally drained. But I still love the taste of muscadines—when I pop one in my mouth, the sweet burst is like a taste of freedom.

. . .

In the Graham jail, the only time you got out of your cell was for church on Saturdays or visitations on Sundays. A woman named Annie Mae Dickie came in to play the piano, and a few people from the Gideon organization performed the church service. The music was the best part. I loved to sing. When I was young, I would pat out a beat on my legs, or a table—anywhere I could, really—and I'd try to get my sisters to sing along with me. Sometimes it was a song we all knew from the radio; other times, I just made up my own songs and tried to teach them the words.

I shared a cell for a while with this guy Fearnow. He was a white guy with red hair and freckles, a small-time thief whose crimes probably had more to do with boredom than a criminal mind. He had been caught breaking and entering, and after he was arrested, he broke down in the interrogation room and confessed to a whole bunch more B and E's. Sixty-four counts in total. He was crazy for a girl named Wendy, so crazy in love that the thought of being separated from her for whatever time he was going to have to serve was undoing him. One night, I woke just as he was about to hang himself. He had slashed his blanket with a razor and braided it into a rope, and he was sweating buckets and sobbing. I talked him down the best I could. "It's not worth it, man. You wanna never see her again? You can't kill yourself and put that on her. What's she gonna do?"

We were tight after that. But about a month in, my court-appointed attorney, Mr. Moseley, told me that Fearnow had given a statement to the police. "Says you were talking in your sleep," Moseley explained. "Says he heard you mumbling, 'Shut up or I'll cut you. It's been a long time, baby, your man's in Germany, ain't he?' "

I guess Fearnow was trying to make himself a deal. I had made the mistake of telling him about the lineup.

· · ·

The week after my arrest, they brought me back to the station for a lineup, where I was told to walk forward, turn 180 degrees to the right, and then read a statement off a card: "Shut up or I'll cut you! Hey, baby, how ya doing? Your man's over in Germany. It's been a long time." There were seven of us standing there; I was number five. The detectives and my attorney, Phil, stood in the back of the room, while some of the officers were sitting down with Ms. Thompson. There was no partition, and I could see she was young, blond, and trying to act tough. When I walked forward, I was so nervous I messed up and said, "Shut up or I'll kill you!"

Ms. Thompson whispered something to Detective Gauldin and they asked me and number four, standing next to me, to repeat the process. This time I got it right. "Shut up or I'll cut you!" I said my bit and then stepped back in line. It was like facing the firing squad. *Please don't pick me,* I thought. I know they said she identified me from my photograph, but now that she saw me in person, I thought maybe she'd see I wasn't the right guy. It would have been all over then.

Ms. Thompson wrote something down on a piece of paper and slipped it to Detective Gauldin. Gauldin pushed his chair back and brought it over to show to my attorney. I could feel my heart up in my throat. Phil looked at the piece of paper and dropped his head. I knew it then. She had picked me. My hands started sweating and my legs got real wobbly.

Ms. Thompson left the room with Gauldin, and in a little while, they brought in the second victim, Ms. Reynolds. They made us do it again for her. I was like a robot. Ms. Reynolds was a lot older than Ms. Thompson, and she wasn't trying to be tough. She was crying and crying and getting hysterical. She wrote something on a piece of paper and detectives led her out of the room. Later on, Phil told me she picked out the guy standing next to me, number four, a college student who lived not too far from the Brookwood apartments who wasn't a real suspect. He also told me we had trouble.

"You want to tell me again where you were on July twenty-eighth, and the early morning hours of the twenty-ninth?" Phil said.

I sighed, explaining that I'd mixed up my days.

"Ronald, it's going to look like you lied."

"I'm not lying. I didn't do it."

But it didn't matter. I was a goner as long as Jennifer Thompson sat there pointing the finger at me. "Yeah, you're innocent," smirked the guards at the jail. "You and everyone else here, right, Cotton?" It was a big joke.

• • •

On August 28, I saw Jennifer Thompson again. I went before the court for a probable cause hearing, where they were trying to determine the severity of the charges and whether to turn it over to Superior Court. My attorney had requested bond reduction on the pending charges, but after Jennifer Thompson took the stand

and recounted what happened to her, the judge increased the bond on each individual charge to a total of $450,000 and ruled the case would go to Superior Court.

I'll never forget that judge spinning around in his chair—if looks could kill, I'd have been dead then. And maybe better off. With that bond, I was going to remain in Alamance County Jail in Graham until the trial. I turned twenty-three four days before Christmas inside that jail. My whole life was supposed to be ahead of me, but my life looked like it was already over.

The trial started in January. Every day, I'd go back and forth between the county jail and the big courthouse in Graham. In the courtroom, I sat and listened while Phil tried to argue that the woman had made a mistake. He told the judge that the jurors should know about the other woman who had been attacked that night but didn't pick me out of the lineup, even though the police said it was the same guy. But the judge said no. The judge also said no to Phil's request to put a memory expert in front of the jury, to testify about how you think you can see something, and be sure, but still be wrong. So it wasn't a total surprise when Phil showed up at the county jail and asked me if I wanted to think about pleading out.

He stood outside the holding cell I was in. It was bigger than the regular cells, about ten by twelve, and painted kind of pink. The idea was that it helped with your attitude when you were going in and out of the courtroom.

"Ron, we've got to face the fact here that there's a good chance you'll get convicted," he said. "I ran into the district attorney at lunch. Do you want me to see if we might be able to get a plea bargain?"

He looked out at me from under his dark brows and waited.

Despite the bars all around me, I was an innocent man. God knew it, and I knew it, and I would rather die incarcerated than admit to being the rapist they claimed I was. Besides, look what pleading guilty the last time to attempted rape as a juvenile did: Everyone threw it back in my face, and it was one of the main reasons Phil advised me not to take the stand. I told him I wanted to explain my side of things, that I had gotten my dates confused in the beginning when the police asked for my alibi. But Phil said the inconsistent alibi would only give the D.A. the opportunity to brand me as a liar.

"No," I told him. "I'm not pleading guilty to something I didn't do."

"Okay, Ron," Phil said. "Okay."

He didn't pressure me to go for a plea bargain the way my other attorney had, though I could see in his eyes it would have been a relief if I had.

Instead, we went on with the trial. Phil, always in a perfect suit and perfect tie, argued the best he could. I sat and listened, sometimes bringing my hand to my face; I'd rest my thumb on my chin and my index finger on my mouth, having to stay silent when everyone was just telling a pack of lies about me.

• • •

During the trial, I would steal a few glances at Jennifer Thompson, thinking, *Why? Why are you doing this?* She just stared back at me with hate. She rolled her eyes at me. The jurors, the DAs, the cops—all of them looked at me like I was something they wanted to spit at and stomp into the ground. In response, I adopted the guarded look I learned long ago when dealing with the authorities, when it seemed like they could do or say whatever they wanted, regardless. I knew I was goner: I just didn't know how bad it was going to be.

On January 18, 1985, I was sentenced to life in prison plus fifty years. I stood there as the judge read my sentence. He called me one of the most dangerous men he had ever met; the district attorney said I was a "menace to society." I could scarcely look at anyone, but I caught a glimpse of my mom and some of my sisters who were able to make it to court that day. They were stunned, like someone had just slapped them. I pinched my right arm as hard as I could. The crescent indent marks on my skin appeared just as the court officers moved in to take me away: This was a nightmare I couldn't wake up from.

CHAPTER 6

NOW THAT THE WORST had happened, I wanted to get it over with. I didn't want to waste any more time in that god-awful jail. If the rest of my life was going to be in state prison, I wanted to get on with it, whatever it was going to be. Later that day, I wrote a letter to the jailer. "Sir," I wrote. "I've been locked up for a crime I didn't commit. I've been tried, convicted, and sentenced. And I'm ready to go on to serve the sentence. If I don't get out of here, I'm going to start tearing the place apart."

· · ·

The next morning an officer came to my cell and told me to get my things together; they were taking me to the penitentiary. It was a clear January morning when we drove up to Central Prison, just past downtown Raleigh. It really hit me then, facing that big

---

brick building with a razor-wire-topped fence all around it: There was no way out.

We had to stop at the gate, because only corrections officers can carry weapons inside. The officer inside the gatehouse logged in the vehicle, then my driver turned over his gun. They put it in a holding box and searched the car. The big double gates slid open, like the mouth to hell opening wide to swallow me up. Once we drove in, they took me out of the car and I was walked into the receiving office. They took anything left from my civilian life and put it in a box; I showered and then was sprayed with a disinfectant just like a dog getting defleaed.

I changed into my prison clothes: tan shirt, pants, and a T-shirt, and took the extra set they gave me and my bed linens. Thankfully, I had my own sneakers. If you couldn't afford your own, they issued you cheap white and black shoes that we called "fish heads," on account of their being so pointy. I got into an elevator and went up to the second floor. There they fingerprinted me and took my picture. A guard escorted me down a long corridor that connected the buildings, then through a door to the yard. The other inmates were standing around screaming, "Fresh meat!" and "Hey, pretty boy, I got something for you." I was shaking in my thin prison outfit, but I flipped them the bird. I had lost a lot of weight in the Graham jail—so much that my mom called me a broom handle. But I tried to stand tall, to square my shoulders. Scared as I was, this was no place to show it.

•   •   •

I was just one of the thousands of people who pass through Central's double gates—it's a "point of entry" into the system for men twenty-two years and older who have sentences of at least twenty years. I was on the young side of the population, which housed some of the worst offenders in the state. North Carolina uses Central Prison to diagnose how well you are going to fit, how well you are going to do in the corrections system. But for me, it just felt like the point of no return. How could anyone survive here?

When I got to the dormitory, there were about six cots in the room, double bunked. The guard told me to take one of the middle bunks, which had been stripped bare. I set about making the bed. This was a temporary dorm filled with the most recent inmates who were still waiting to be processed and assigned permanently. Somebody wandered in.

"What up, man? What's your name?"

"Cotton," I replied, short enough to hope it ended the conversation there.

"How long you got?"

"Life plus fifty," I said, not looking at him.

"Whatcha in for?" he pressed on.

Finally, I turned to face him. "Look, man, it's none of your business. I don't want to be bothered right now."

He left the room and I laid down on my bunk. It felt like even God had forgotten about me. The weight of the world was on me, sucking me down into a darkness I didn't think I could swim out of.

● ● ●

One of the first things they do is assign you to a caseworker, and mine was an old, balding black guy. His head was so shiny the lights reflected off it. Before they can give you a work detail, you have to go through an evaluation period. For two weeks, you go every day and take tests: math tests, spelling tests, personality tests. Dot after dot to fill in. I know some people just filled in anything. The point was to figure out your skills, your education level, and see where they could put you.

"Where do you think you might like to work?" my caseworker asked me when all the tests were done.

"The kitchen," I told him. I had had plenty of experience working in kitchens on the outside after I quit school, and besides, I knew it meant you could eat your meals away from the rest of the population, hopefully away from trouble. I chose it even though some of the people I had started to get friendly with didn't think I should get a job in the kitchen because New York was there.

New York was a big guy who had been in for about fifteen years. He wore a knit cap on his head no matter what the weather was. In the chow hall, he grinned at me and put extra food on my plate. "You a skinny little thing," he said, winking. But I knew the game. He thought he was going to get some. He'd been shooting his mouth off about me, telling people I was his. I was determined not to break.

• • •

In prison, working out and staying strong is a form of surviving. Not only did you need to be able to throw someone down, but also you needed to exhaust yourself or else you might never sleep. Back in the Graham county jail, I would run in place and do sit-ups and push-ups on the floor of the cell, anything to keep myself moving.

But at Central Prison there was a gym, and I went every day. I pressed weights, did push-ups. A friend of mine would spot me as we'd load more and more weight to the bar. When I was younger, people called me "Flat"—I was so skinny there was no backside. Even my mom would call me that. So in here, I tried to eat as much as I could and pack on some muscle. I would do as many repetitions as I could, losing count as I pushed the weight away from me, pushing through the burning and the tearing. Inside my body, things were breaking down so I could build them up. You have to rip your muscles apart before they can get stronger.

One morning, I was on my way to the gym, walking down the long tunnel that separated my dormitory from the exercise area. It was the same corridor they bring you down when they are escorting you to your cell the first time. A corrections officer passed me with a new inmate—I saw him out of the corner of my eye for only a minute. It was one of those minutes that seemed longer than it was because something about him struck me as familiar. It was something I felt all over.

Two days later, I was out in the yard on the handball court and I saw the new inmate again. "Tony," I said to the guy who was watching from the sidelines. "Take my place for a minute. I gotta go check something." I jogged over to the new guy standing there, trying to take it all in. I had been there three months already, but he was just getting his footing, scanning the yard.

I looked at the short hair, the thin mustache, and the mouth that wasn't too wide but was full. He was light skinned, lighter than me. And it flashed in my mind: the composite picture of the suspect in the rapes they pegged me for. I had first seen the sketch in the paper when I was hanging out with my brother Calvin. It had been all over the news. Two white girls got raped in the same night. "Man," I recalled saying to Calvin. "When they get him, he's done."

The guy standing in front of me looked just like him.

"'Scuse me," I said. "Where're you from?"

He turned to me. "Burlington."

"That right? Me, too. I think I've seen you around."

"Yeah?" he said, not sure if he should trust me.

"Name's Cotton. Ron Cotton."

"Bobby Poole," he replied.

"Fact is, you look like the drawing of the suspect in the crime I'm locked up for."

His face gave away nothing.

"Did you have anything to do with it?" I was trying to be real casual, not too confrontational.

He kind of smiled. "Nah, man. Not me."

I walked away and went back to the handball court. Every now and again I'd glance back over at him. His name was Bobby Leon Poole, and he was in here for rape.

I had my suspicions that he was lying to me, but then again, in prison, you can never know for certain who's telling you the truth and who isn't.

CHAPTER 7

I STARTED ON KITCHEN DETAIL sweeping and mopping for forty cents a day on the 4:00 A.M. to 2:00 P.M. shift. The money I earned went into an inmate trust fund, which you could use to buy items like soap or candy bars from the canteen. Thirty dollars was the most you could withdraw at one time from your fund. If you were caught "overloaded"—with more money than that on you—guards would confiscate the overflow. They were trying to prevent loan-sharking and drug dealing. More than a few times you'd see an inmate suddenly offer to go to the commissary and buy you anything you wanted: microwaved sandwiches, hot dogs, cigarettes—anything to keep the corrections officers from getting their hands on the money.

Working in the kitchen had a lot of advantages. Instead of waiting for lockdown and head count before dinner, kitchen workers could eat dinner earlier than the rest of the population. In the chow hall, I tried to keep my distance when I ate with the rest of the kitchen crew. If someone invited me to sit down with him, I would, but I wasn't going to try to make myself fit in. So most of the time, I ate alone. Breakfast was powdered eggs scrambled up, sausage if you were lucky, and juice. They served pizza, hamburgers, or hot dogs with baked beans and a slice of fruit for lunch. Dinner would be meat loaf or some kind of chicken with pinto beans or black-eyed peas. And always milk—we had milk with every meal. Every week, the milk came in big bags delivered from prison farm camps around the state.

The tables in the chow hall were built right into the floor: round metal circles with arms connecting to four or five stools—smaller round circles. The base was set in the shiny concrete floor. If there was a fight, the tables and seats weren't going anywhere. You couldn't pick up a chair or a table to do some serious damage.

One afternoon, New York in his stupid knit hat came over with his tray and sat across from me, knocking my tray with his. He winked at me. *Here we go,* I thought. I knew my reputation in this place would depend on how the next few minutes went down.

"Look, man, the best thing you can do is move away from this table and leave me alone," I said.

He stood up and yelled, "What you gonna do?"

I got up. "You want some? Come on," I said, waving him toward me with my hands. Better to die there in the chow hall, I thought, with my pants on.

Everyone came running over. Some people yelled, "It ain't worth it! It ain't worth it!" while others cheered the fight on. A good fight was entertainment, after all, something to break up the day. Before anything could happen, guards were on us.

New York left me alone after that. But soon I had other problems to deal with.

. . .

"Here comes Red, pretty as a woman. I'm gonna make love to you."

Kenny was a stocky guy from Union County who worked in pots and pans on kitchen detail. He took to calling me "Red" on account of the Indian in me, and the fact that if I was out in the yard too long, I would burn more from the sun than the other black guys did. Also, I didn't have to shave because I didn't have much facial hair, except for a bit of fuzz above my lip.

"Red, your skin is smooth like a girl's," he would say, his full mustache curving down around his big mouth. He had a crease across his forehead so hard it looked like someone could have made it with a knife, and bags under his eyes that made him look a lot older, although I think he only had about three years on me. It seemed like a face trouble had made.

"My name's not Red," I told Kenny repeatedly. "It's Cotton."

"Sure thing, Red," he'd say.

Kenny did karate and was cut from years of lifting. He'd already done five years and, like a lot of guys, pumping all that weight had pumped up his head. He was compact, and always ready to spring into a fight despite a bad leg that made him limp.

He was serving time for kidnapping and rape. Other inmates said he'd gotten convicted because of his body odor. I tried to stay far enough away from him so I wouldn't find out if it was true or not. Besides, I'd always had bad sinus problems that kept my nose stuffed up.

My hair grew long in prison. It was easier, because of the heat and humidity in the kitchen, to manage it if it was plaited. The long hair gave Kenny more reason to taunt me.

After I finished my work shift for the day, I usually went to shower to get the dirty-water smell and the kitchen grease off me. One night, I was rinsing out the shampoo with my hair hanging down over my eyes. Like a spooked dog, alarm shot up the back of my spine. The shower curtain slid aside.

"You got a nice ass for a man."

I lifted the hair from my face and opened one eye to see Kenny standing there with another guy I didn't know.

"Man, you need to take that shit somewhere else," I said, knowing that I couldn't fight. There were two of them and besides, I was butt naked. If I slipped and fell, I'd wake up with a sore rear.

Kenny stood there for a long minute. He made a noise like there was something good to eat. "Mmm, mmm, mmm," he said, smacking his lips before he walked away.

. . .

There was a saying in prison: Keep your mind off the street and your hands off the meat. The second part was easy enough to understand. The first part was harder. To some people, it meant trying to use the time you were doing to get better, to educate yourself, so if you did get back out on the street, you wouldn't do something stupid to wind up back in the penitentiary. Other people, myself included, thought it also had something to do with letting life on the outside go. You couldn't keep thinking about

everything you were missing in your old life. Things on the outside moved on without you.

Inside, you had to adapt to new rules: If you weren't jittery or
on edge, you might miss the blink in the half second before you
got stabbed in the side in the rec room or out in the yard. Or the
way two guys might suddenly close in on you in a corner out
of the CO's line of sight. I kept one eye trained for any sign of
trouble, and with the other I tracked Bobby Poole through Central
Prison.

· · ·

A few days after the shower incident, I was waiting for my turn to
shoot pool down in the exercise room when Roger Blackstock
came in. He was a heavy guy with a large, friendly looking face and
double chin that flowed right into his neck. He wore gold-rimmed
glasses that made him look smart, which he was. Originally from
Greensboro, Roger had been incarcerated for a while, for three
counts of rape. He had a few life sentences but had had one taken
off—he became very knowledgeable about the law and worked on
his case himself. In fact, he looked over other inmates' briefs for
them—he ran sort of an underground legal clinic that Kenny was
part of, too. Roger was like a big brother to a lot of people. He was
president of the Jaycees club there at Central; it was an organization trying to promote being a "model inmate." I trusted him.

Roger had a serious look on his face as he headed straight for
me. "Cotton," he said, "Kenny's been talking about you."

He didn't have to say more. Since Kenny showed up in the
shower, I knew I had to act. Even though Kenny didn't have that

reputation, I couldn't wait to find out if he was all talk. If he surprised me again, I might not be so lucky. And if word spread that Kenny broke me, I'd be a goner. The beginning of your time was very important: the battles you won and lost had everything to do with where you were going to fit in.

I put my pool stick down and walked out of the exercise room, down the long corridor toward the kitchen where Kenny was working. He had his back to me.

"Kenny! Let me holler at you a minute," I said.

He turned around. "Whatcha want, man?"

"You've been talking junk about me ever since I got here and I'm tired of it. I want my name to taste like shit in your mouth." I pushed him toward a rack of pots and pans; he felt as solid and heavy as a tree trunk. I was taller than him but skinnier.

"Cotton, I don't know where you're getting your information from, but you better get outta my face before I kill you." He shoved me back.

"Let's go!"

I headed around a corner out of the guard's line of sight. I looked at the wet floor and realized my steel-toed brogans would give me no traction. I hurried to get them off, but I was still down on one knee messing with my right shoe when Kenny surprised me with a roundhouse. He kicked me upside the head near my left eye. Like one of those old-time flashbulbs, pain exploded in a white burst before I was able to partially block his foot with my hand. I scrambled to my feet, my face burning and wet with blood, and punched him in the throat. I knocked the wind out of him for a minute. I could hear him gasping for air even as he kept coming at me.

He grabbed at my shirt, trying to pull it up over my head so I couldn't see. The shirt ripped instead, splitting apart like a busted zipper until I just had two flaps hanging on my back.

Kenny quickly got his meaty hands around my neck, squeezing it hard. I got my forearm around the back of his legs and knocked him to the floor, going down with him. I heard the guards' whistle and the sound of running footsteps. Next thing I knew, Roger was pulling me away from Kenny and a corrections officer grabbed Kenny.

Roger still had me by the arms when the CO released Kenny. Seeing his chance, Kenny went for me like he was going to do me in. I sprang up on my toes and kicked him. The CO who'd held him moved in quickly and dragged Kenny away, while another CO took me into the kitchen stewards' office.

"You OK?" asked Mr. Dunn, one of the older stewards.

I nodded at him, trying to catch my breath.

"What's the problem, Cotton? Why y'all fighting, anyway?"

"Kenny's been bothering me ever since I got here. I was just defending myself."

Mr. Dunn sighed. It wasn't anything new to him, I guess.

"Yeah, but you know the rules. An infraction like this is gonna mean lockdown, whoever started it. Look, your face is all bloody. Let's get you to the hospital."

The skin above my eye had torn open as easily as my shirt had, but they bandaged it up well. Another CO came in to tell me it was time to get ready for lockup. He brought me to a holding cell and another officer came in with a grievance form. "Fill this out," he said. "Then we'll move you to Cell Block C. I gotta go and check on something."

C—or lockdown—is the prison within the prison, the place

where they house the worst of the worst who can't be with the rest of the population. When you're in that unit, you get out of your cell once a week for an hour outside. Out in the yard, there's a thing that looks like a batting cage. One at a time, that's where locked-down inmates got their exercise and sun.

The CO returned about twenty minutes later. "Cotton, go change your shirt and get to work," he said. "A steward told us he heard Kenny talking. I hope you taught that fag a lesson."

Kenny got lockdown for thirty days.

• • •

Dec. 1, 1985

Mr. Moseley,

I've been waiting patiently to hear from you before now but I assume, being an attorney, you've been extremely busy. Well, it's going on a year now that I've been incarcerated here at Central Prison, and I haven't received any documents concerning my case or much less know how things look on my behalf.

Mr. Moseley, it's hell living here. It's as though I'm left without anything to look forward to. I'm lost and don't know what's happening, but perhaps you can tell me.

Sincerely,
Ronald Cotton

• • •

Bobby Poole took a job in the kitchen, but I didn't interact with him. I just continued to monitor him. He had hospital detail, packaging the meals to deliver to inmates in the prison hospital. One of the kitchen stewards, Mr. Chauncy, could never tell us apart.

"Hey, Poole!" he always said to me.

"I'm not Poole," I'd say, spitting his name out. "I'm Cotton." It really irritated me.

In the trial, my attorney had tried to say it was mistaken identity. And here was proof. If even the guards in prison couldn't tell us apart, how could the victims of the crime? I had a callus on my finger from all the letters I wrote to TV stations, newspapers, legal organizations, and of course, my attorney, Phil Moseley. If anyone besides Phil read any of them, I never knew. I only heard from my family and, occasionally, Phil. I always liked Phil, because he had an honest-looking face. Every time I saw him, he was suited up and dressy, and he never acted as if, even though he was appointed to represent me by the court, I wasn't getting his all. Phil didn't beat around the bush, either, and I appreciated that. Phil told me he and Dan Monroe, the other lawyer who helped out on my case, would appeal my conviction on the grounds that evidence about the second woman, Ms. Reynolds, who was raped that night but did not identify me in the lineup, should have been allowed in. The cops were sure it was the same guy who attacked both women. So if they were so certain I was that rapist, why would they try to hide Ms. Reynolds's evidence?

· · ·

"Cotton!" I heard someone hollering outside my window, as I lay on my bunk listening to R & B with my headphones on.

I looked up and saw Kenny looking in. *Oh, shit.*

"Can I speak to you for a moment?" he said.

I got off my bunk and motioned for him to sit in one of the chairs I had lining the wall.

"Look, man, I'm sorry for fighting with you. I'd like us to be friends."

"You sure got a strange way of showing it," I said.

"Cotton, I've been helping out Poole with his case. He's been trying to get back into court and asked me to help him out, look over his papers and stuff. He told me he did the crimes you're in for."

Like Roger, Kenny studied law all the time. Other inmates would go to him for legal advice. But I didn't trust Kenny. He was being too nice to me. I thought he might be trying to set me up, so I played it cool.

"That right?" I said.

"Yeah, man, just thought you'd wanna know."

I nodded and told him thanks. I wondered what kind of trick he was trying to pull. But maybe Poole had admitted something to him. After he left my cell, I got out a legal pad and pen to make some notes for Phil. Poole was a rapist from Burlington, and even the guards couldn't tell us apart. What if Jennifer Thompson picked the wrong guy? If we could prove Poole did it, I'd go free.

In the next few weeks, whenever I passed Poole in the hallways, it was as if we were in a Western. I was always ready to spin around on my heels and take him on. I watched him as close as I could without letting him know.

• • •

As low as you might sink sometimes, you never let family see you that way. When I knew I had a visit coming up, I'd take my neatest clothes and crease my pants between slats of cardboard, then slide them under my mattress so I could sleep on them for a few nights and press them. I'd comb my hair out with a plastic fork. It was important to show your family you were taking care of yourself; they had enough to worry about.

One Sunday when we were heading back to the dorms after visiting hours were over, Poole came up to me. I was briefly shocked, to be standing face to face with the man I was now convinced had me serving his time.

"Hey, Cotton. That your sister?" he said, nodding in the direction of the visitation area, where my baby sister Shelia had just left.

"Yeah," I said.

"What's her name?"

"Susie," I lied. We actually called her Pig, much as she hated it, but she was stuck with the name since she was small, when she'd had a habit of chewing the corners of her schoolbooks.

"I might like to write her. Give me her address," he said, grinning at me like he was Prince Charming.

I didn't want him having contact with any of my family. But I played along.

"She won't write to just anybody, man. Not someone she doesn't even know. But we could take a picture, and I'll send it to her, let her know of your interest, and I'll tell you what she says. OK?"

Poole bought it, and later that week when members of the Jaycee club came around, offering to take a Polaroid for two dollars, we had someone take a picture of us standing side by side. I was at least five inches taller than him. But I didn't send it to Shelia. I sent it to Phil.

Sept. 30, 1986

Mr. Moseley, there is no doubt in my mind that Bobby Poole did the crime I'm serving time for. I work in the kitchen here with him. Mr. Moseley, as I've said before, Poole is the one. I've enclosed a picture of Poole and me. Maybe you could use it . . .

. . .

My sister Diane called, informing me our mother had had a stroke, leaving her temporarily paralyzed and unable to see. I couldn't help but think that my situation had put her there: Her blood pressure may have been sky high, but watching your son get labeled a rapist and hauled off to the penitentiary must be very stressful. If she died, I might not even get to go to her funeral, and even if I did go, I'd be in handcuffs with a corrections officer by my side.

Diane asked me to pray for her, but instead I allowed the anger and the frustration to grow. The cops had set me up, I thought, because I had dated white women. I'd never raped anybody. I was furious at the woman who said I raped her, at the DA, the judge, the cops, who were keeping me from my family when they needed me. I was sure they were all home with their families, and they didn't give a damn about another black man rotting in prison. It didn't even matter to them if they had the right one. I thought about Jennifer Thompson, Detective Sully, Detective Gauldin, and Detective Lowe as I pounded the punching bag. I didn't care if I broke my fingers.

Rage ate at me like a cancer. I could scream and shatter my own eardrums, but no one else heard me. The rules were different if you were a black man. What the cops and the DA and the victim said mattered, and what I said, didn't. I had heard nothing from even Phil. I felt that I had no hope. I would die in a cell like an abandoned dog at a kennel for something someone else did. And it didn't bother the man who really committed the crimes one bit.

· · ·

A few weeks later, Poole was transferred to my dorm. I knew I had to do something then.

After work at night, I'd take a hot shower, lie in my bunk, and think. There was no way out for me. If I couldn't get justice, maybe I should just take it. A loose piece of metal on the edge of a desk gave me an answer. I pried it off and quickly put it in my pants. Later, I took a T-shirt and rolled it up tight with some duct tape and made a handle.

My father came in from Hillsborough to pay me a visit. Dad's name was James (everyone called him Jimmy), and he had lots of kids, including some sons I never even knew about until I met them later in prison. He never married my mother; he had married someone else, so I never lived with him. But Dad had his favorites and I was one of them. A lot of people never knew who their daddy was, or even if they knew, their fathers weren't around. But my father tried to be with us as much as he could. My brother Terry even told me once he envied me, because he saw my father more than he saw his own.

My father had a hot temper and liked his liquor. He drove around with a shotgun and a dark bottle of brandy on the floor of his two-door black '51 Ford. When we were small, we were in a wreck with him. I recall Mom was doing Diane's hair in the living room. Dad came in drunk and said he wanted to take us kids for a ride. My mother asked him how much he had been drinking. They started arguing and my father made me, Calvin, and Diane get in the car with him. My brother and sister sat in the back; I was in the front seat. Dad sped along a dirt road in Caswell County and flipped the car. I got thrown out the open window and landed in the cow pasture, right next to a cow named Big Ben. My father went through the windshield and got cut up real bad. The backseat came loose and my brother and sister ended up in the trunk. Diane broke her arm and Calvin had a lot of knocks on his head. After that, my father slowed down drinking a bit. He might not have been perfect, but he was there for us. He loved us, and he made sure we knew it.

If anyone would understand why I thought my only choice was to kill Poole, I thought it would be him. I told my father my intentions. I didn't let him know I had already made a weapon, I just told him I wanted to take Poole out. He fixed me with his eyes through the Plexiglas window in the visitors' room.

"Ron, you told me you were innocent of this crime and I believed you, but if you take this man's life, you ain't never coming home. You'll belong in here."

When the visit ended, I thought about what he said all the way back to my cell. Was I the same as the guys in lockdown, the guys who felt nothing putting a shiv into a man already in prison?

I had written letter after letter, waiting for news on the appeal, hoping some newspaper would pick up my story. I was tired of waiting. I wanted something to happen. All I could do was take Poole's life. He had taken mine away. But once I killed someone, chances were I'd be killed, too—marked.

After lights-out that night, I took my weapon from under my mattress where I had hidden it, and clutched it to my chest, thinking about Poole sleeping easy, fifteen feet away. I stayed awake all night, imagining what my mother would do, or Diane, or Tudy, or Shelia. They all loved me and visited when they could. They believed in me, wrote me letters of support. Would they still love me if I was a killer? Would my sisters still bring my nephews to visit, and say, "There's your Uncle Ron"? I got out a pencil and scribbled in the dark a letter I never sent: "Mom," I wrote, "This place is turning me into a madman, turning me into someone I don't want to be. It's making me want to hurt myself, hurt other people . . ."

In the morning, I decided I didn't want to go out on a stretcher. I wanted to walk out someday, the same way I went in. I was no angel, but I wasn't a murderer. I could have easily sold my weapon for thirty or forty dollars, but that would just mean someone else would die. I had to get rid of it fast before I changed my mind. I took the shank to a kitchen drain in the floor, one with a loose cover, and dropped it down, then waited until I heard the clink it made when it landed.

CHAPTER 8

SHORTLY AFTER I threw away my weapon, Bobby Leon Poole was transferred out to another prison. I got word of it through a buddy of mine in the kitchen who spotted his name on the transfer list. Kitchen staff got the list every week because they'd have to prepare special meals for inmates getting shipped out. While it was still dark, guards escorted the transfers to the kitchen, and by five or six in the morning, they were on a bus bound for Sandy Ridge, the transfer terminal. Even though Poole's Cheshire Cat grin no longer taunted me in the halls of Central, he remained on my mind.

To anyone on the outside, Poole and I were the same. Rapists. Animals. I guess that's what my father meant when he said if I killed Poole, I'd belong here. Innocence wouldn't matter anymore if I had his blood on my hands. Letting go of the weapon was one of the first important decisions I made. There wasn't much I could control about the way my life was going, but I could control whether I let my rage get the best of me. I knew, even if no one else did, that I was not the same type of man as Bobby Poole. I would not go to my grave knowing I let someone else waste away for something I did.

One morning, coming back from the gym, as I walked along the corridor, I heard a group of guys harmonizing some music. Even in this place, their voices sounded joyful. I wandered up to the band room and stood in the back, listening.

A dark-skinned older guy named John Kelly came over to me. He had his hair in neat cornrows, and there was a bit of gray in them. His mouth was so wide that when he smiled, he was all teeth.

The teeth smiled and said to me, "Want to participate?"

I told him I would. They made some room for me and asked me if I knew "Will the Circle Be Unbroken?" I nodded and joined in.

> *Will the circle be unbroken?*
> *By and by, Lord, by and by,*
> *There's a better home a-waitin'*
> *In the sky, Lord, in the sky.*

• • •

At the beginning of my second year, I received a letter from Phil Moseley. The Supreme Court in North Carolina had overturned my conviction, entitling me to a new trial back in Alamance County. Turns out, they agreed it was a mistake that the evidence about the other rape—the fact that the woman couldn't pick me in the lineup when they knew it had to have been the same person—should have been allowed in the trial. Hope inflated in me like a balloon, carrying me through long shifts in the kitchen and the stretches between visits from my family. I continued to sing with the choir, my voice rising up out of the hundred-year-old walls of Central Prison. Maybe it even reached God, because it seemed like my luck was changing. Diane told me my mother's condition improved, and she also told me she had been praying. "Ron, you're coming out of there. The good Lord spoke to me and showed me a sign," Diane wrote. "I've been telling everybody and they think I'm crazy. 'Sister Cotton's gone crazy,' they say. But you're coming out of there."

We'd all come up Baptist, although most of us slipped along the way. When we were kids, we hated having it shoved down our throats. But I did reach for the Bible while I was incarcerated. At first, it was more like homesickness that made me pick it up. I read it because it was familiar—and almost always available in the penitentiary.

My father and Diane were always on me to take up prayer. "The Lord is going to be there for you when no one else is, son. When no one else is listening, he will lean down his ear," said my father, sounding every bit like a Sunday preacher. In his later years, he'd curbed his drink and even became a deacon at his church.

· · ·

The new trial would begin in November 1987, but I got sent back to Graham nine months before that to prepare. Like a film projector running backward, the scenes played in reverse: in February

1987, there I was, back in the county jail awaiting trial. Only this time, there was a new facility on Maple Street in Graham. Unlike the old jail, where officers did rounds, they had a guard stationed in a booth assigned to every dorm, watching prisoners around the clock. It was as close to home as I had been in three years.

My father, Diane, Tudy, Shelia, and some of my other sisters visited when they could. Only my mother did not make it to visit me in jail. "Joe's been hard on her lately," one of my sisters told me, talking about my mom's boyfriend. "And besides that, the stroke left her weak. She's saving her strength up for court, Ron. She's going to be there, God willing." My mother wrote me, sending me notes with shaky handwriting. Phil and Dan dropped by now and again, to go over legal documents. On the days I did not have visitors, I simply waited for any kind of news, with a mixture of uncertainty about what would happen in trial and hope that the truth would finally come out to keep me company.

Early one morning, a female jailer who sometimes handled the mail delivered some papers. "You've got to be in court tomorrow morning," she said.

I didn't look at them, figuring they must have been something official saying the state charged me with the rape of Jennifer Thompson in Alamance County. But later on, while I was playing cards out in the day room with another guy, I happened to glance down at them on the floor. The name "Mary Reynolds" jumped out at me. I dropped the cards, revealing my hand, and picked up the papers.

"What man? What's up?"

"My case," I said, reading and trying to understand what was happening. Hope drained from me along with the color in my face.

"Man, you don't look so good."

Three and a half years after the fact, Mary Reynolds, the second victim, said she recognized me as the man who attacked her. She claimed she knew it was me all along but had been too afraid during the lineup to identify me. They were charging me with her rape, too. Just like that, my problems doubled.

"They're charging me with another rape," I told him.

"When they want you, they will get you," he said, and I knew he was right. If it was so important to the community that a black man be punished for these crimes, I guess any one would do, so they pinned it on me.

That night in my cell I read from the Book of Psalms: "Deliver me not over unto the will of mine enemies: for false witnesses are risen up against me, and such as breathe out cruelty." All I could think was that now that I had a chance at getting out with this new trial, the cops had gotten this woman to change her story. *Why, God?* I asked. *Why me?*

• • •

The new ADA, Luke Turner, was black, which worried me. He'd have more to prove. I'd seen it happen before: you work with some guy and then he gets promoted over you and suddenly he's worse than any white boss you ever had. In court the next day, the judge decided there was enough evidence to proceed with the charges in the rape of Mary Reynolds and officially appointed Dan Monroe co-counsel to represent me. Dan had helped Phil during the first trial, too, but he mostly sat back at the table observing, lodging objections. It was unusual, Phil said, for me to have two lawyers, but I guess it spoke to how difficult my case was.

The news that I would be prosecuted for two rapes hit me like a sucker punch, sneaking up and popping me when I least expected it. The cops and prosecutors might think they were better than all the men they locked up, but this kind of blow was exactly what you'd get in prison. The state made a "motion for joinder"—to consolidate the two rape cases together instead of having two separate trials—and the court allowed it.

• • •

As Phil and Dan prepared for trial, they became very interested in Bobby Poole. They agreed that the picture I sent them showed similarities in the way we looked, similarities to the composite, and they found out that the Burlington police had shot Poole in the leg outside the Brookwood Garden apartments the day they'd caught him fleeing from a woman's apartment. It was the same complex Jennifer Thompson lived in when she was assaulted.

I told them about Kenny coming to me and telling me Poole admitted it to him. Phil and Dan went to Central Prison to interview Kenny.

• • •

The night before the trial began, I kneeled down beside my bunk. *Dear Heavenly Father, you know and I know that I'm an innocent man. Please reveal this miscarriage of justice during the new trial. Please protect me and give me strength to endure, and please protect my loved ones.*

The first thing Phil and Dan tried to do was make sure that the two women who said I attacked them were not in the courtroom at the same time. I thought this was very important, because otherwise Mary Reynolds would hear Jennifer Thompson testify and she'd make sure her story matched up. When the judge denied that motion, I didn't think we were off to a good start. But it was nothing compared to what happened when they selected the jury.

Four black people from the community got called in for jury duty. The judge, himself, dismissed one of them, and then Mr. Turner made sure none of the rest sat on my jury. Dan and Phil tried to move for a mistrial, right at the beginning, because of that.

The motion was recorded as follows: "Mr. Cotton's right to trial by a fair and impartial jury has been violated by the prosecutor's use of his peremptory challenges to systematically exclude blacks from the jury. If the record could reflect, your honor, that there were four black jurors in the jury venire. . . . If the record would further reflect that Mr. Turner—who I'll be the first to concede, is also black—he might want that on record, exercised his six—all six, I believe, of his peremptory challenges, but he used three of them to exclude [the above-mentioned black jurors], and the record would further reflect that the [fourth] potential [black] juror, was acquainted with Mr. Turner's family," Dan argued.

"He did not exclude his—use his peremptory challenge to exclude her, although your honor excluded her as a challenge—not as a challenge, because your honor excluded her. So we just simply make that motion, at this time, if your honor please, for a mistrial on the grounds that the systematic exclusion of blacks by the prosecutor, and let the record further reflect, of course, that Mr. Cotton is black—prohibited him from a trial by a jury of his peers, a fair and impartial jury . . ."

"Mr. Turner, will you be heard?" the judge asked.

"Under case law, I am required to respond and give some neutral reason for excluding the blacks from the jury venire. Again, with 'Mr. Johnson,' who stated he knew Mr. Cotton, had been friends with him at an earlier time. 'Mr. Ryan,' whom—he did not remember me, but I am acquainted with him, and also acquainted with his family, who have had various and sundry contacts with the DA's office. 'Ms. Smith,' who knew almost Mr. Cotton's entire family, and her mother was presently living next door to Mr. Cotton's mother; she had gone to school with his aunt and knew his sister, but steadfastly maintained that she could be fair and impartial; and the state did not see fit to take that risk, under the circumstances. I have nothing to say as to 'Ms. Haliwell.'"

Seemed like a bunch of weak excuses to me. It's not like Ms. Smith was a close family friend. I didn't recognize her myself. And how about Mr. Ryan? The guy said he didn't remember Mr. Turner, but since Turner said he knew him, that's what they went with. It was just more proof to me that in the court, only certain people's voices were heard. You'd think Burlington was so small that the only six black people in the courtroom all knew one another. Please.

"Could the record just reflect that the net result was that it's an all-white jury, plus the two alternates are white, your honor?" Dan continued.

The judge agreed to put it on the record, but he denied the motion. The opening arguments hadn't even started, and already I was very worried.

. . .

The next morning, I went into the dressing room at the county jail to change into civilian clothes for court. A man getting ready in the corner turned around, and my heart almost fell out of my mouth. Standing there was Bobby Poole.

He walked over to me.

"Why you have me here?" he said.

"*I* don't have you here, man. My attorneys have you here." I turned and tried to go about my business, playing dumb. Bailiffs entered and escorted him out.

Several minutes later, Kenny walked in. We nodded at each other in acknowledgment.

"Cotton, you got any deodorant? Can I borrow some?"

"Keep it," I said, tossing him an extra roll-on I had. I noticed he was already perspiring, nervous.

"Look, man, I don't know if I can do this. You know what happens to snitches, right? They don't last too long."

"So you're telling me you'd lie for a guilty man? You'd help a guilty man instead of an innocent one?" I said to him. "I'm not asking you to lie. Just tell the truth."

Kenny must have had some kind of conscience to come and tell me about Poole's confession. My only hope was to appeal to his conscience again: Being labeled an informer or not, would he really be able to live with himself, knowing he helped convict an innocent man? What if he was in my shoes?

Kenny thought about it for a few minutes, and nodded. I doubted Kenny was the only person Poole had confessed to, but Kenny was the only person who came forward to me. Despite everything that had happened between us, he earned my respect that day. What he was doing was dangerous, but it was the right thing to do.

I shook his hand.

. . .

In the courtroom, I saw my mother. She leaned over the railing to hug and kiss me and my heart nearly broke to see her condition. She'd lost a lot of weight, and when she took the stand later, she had a lot of trouble remembering things. Their questioning easily confused her, as if her mind was slipping, and I felt bad for my poor mother to have to sit through it at all. They tried to make it out as if she was telling tales to protect her son, instead of treating her like an older woman not in good health.

On the prosecutor's side, they were both there, seated in different rows: Mary Reynolds and Jennifer Thompson. If I so much as glanced in the direction of Jennifer Thompson, I could feel her burn-in-hell glare. Mary Reynolds, on the other hand, seemed desperate to avoid eye contact.

Jennifer Thompson took the stand first. She was more determined than ever. No matter how Phil tried to undo her, she was strong. She had gotten a very good look at her attacker, she said. There was no doubt in her mind. And once again, she confidently picked me out as her rapist.

I had only seen Mary Reynolds once before, during the lineup, so I studied her here in the court. She was much taller than Jennifer Thompson—probably about five foot seven—and she was middle-aged. On the witness stand, she had a really hard time describing what had happened to her. She stopped several times to take off her glasses and wipe her eyes.

Like Jennifer Thompson, Mary Reynolds had been asleep when someone had broken in. She'd woken up on her couch to discover someone was shining a flashlight in her face, groping her. When she'd screamed, he'd walked out the back door. She'd gone into her bedroom and seen everything thrown all around the room, then noticed the window was open. When she had gone over to close it, he'd grabbed at her through the window, pulling her top down. She had tried to close the window but it had been stuck. She described him as a light-skinned black man with short hair and a pin-line mustache, who wore a blue shirt with white stripes. Through the window, he'd grinned at her. *Poole,* I thought, *she's describing Bobby Poole and that smirk he always had.*

Poole had taunted her, I thought, *getting off on her fear.*

She said she had screamed and run out of the bedroom to the phone, trying to call her father, but after ringing once, the line had gone dead. Then Poole had broken through the locked front door and dragged her to another bedroom, where he'd thrown her on the bed. When Mary had tried to fight back, Poole had just knocked her down. There in the wide-open, bright courtroom, I could picture Poole in my mind laughing when Mary recalled that she told her attacker that her husband was coming. "You don't have a husband," I could hear him saying, the same way he said to me, "Nah, man, it wasn't me," after I asked him if he had anything to do with the crimes I'd served time for. He'd shoved a pillow over her mouth to keep her from talking. He'd gone down on her and then raped her, running away when car lights had shone through the open front door.

Poole had really messed her up. That was obvious.

"Is that man in this courtroom today?"

"Yes, sir," Mary Reynolds answered, sobbing.

"Where is he?"

She wouldn't look me in the eye but just motioned over. "He's sitting right there—Ronald Cotton."

I could feel the jury turn and look at me, every single one of their white faces thinking, "You sick motherfucker."

I shook my head. I couldn't believe that this is what people thought of me. I wanted to ask Mary Reynolds, Does it make you feel better to think I'm behind bars? Do you sleep at night, thinking you're safe? If only you knew, Mary, Poole did this to both of us. To all of us.

Phil cross-examined her, pointing out that in her statement, she told Detective Lowe her attacker was five foot nine. Now she said he was five foot nine to six foot. I'm almost six foot four. That's a big difference. She also told Lowe she didn't get a good look at her assailant, which is why the police never asked her to do a composite. I wanted to jump up from the defense table and stand next to her, to show her how much taller I was. But I know the bailiff would have taken me down with a club in a second. It was strange to sit there, the center of attention I never wanted, everyone talking about you as if they know exactly who you are. They pointed at me and stared from a safe distance, like I was a lion at the zoo who'd eat them alive if I got a chance. Inside, I felt like a lamb about to be slaughtered.

Phil drilled into her about the lighting in the apartment, and began to tear apart how much she really did see the man who assaulted her. She maintained that she picked another man in the physical lineup because she was terrified by the seven black men standing in front of her and just wanted to get out of the room, even though she knew I was the one who did it.

Only she never told anyone in law enforcement that she saw me—her supposed rapist—in the lineup until October 30, 1987. Three years after the lineup and right before my re-trial for Jennifer Thompson's rape. What a crock. Someone must have gotten to her, I guessed, made sure I was kept off the streets.

My only hope was that when they saw Bobby Poole, they'd recognize him. They'd realize they made a mistake. But the judge wasn't sure the testimony concerning Poole was going to be allowed in. He held something called a "voir dire" hearing, which Phil explained meant he would have to put up all the evidence about Poole before the judge, but not the jury. The jury would be sent out first, and then it would be up to the judge to decide whether any of that evidence was admissible to the jury. I did not have a good feeling, considering this judge had already decided that there was no problem with an all-white jury's judging me and had allowed the two women to sit in the courtroom the whole time, listening to each other's testimony.

• • •

"Leave the jury out. Bring in the witness," the judge said.

And then Phil said, "I call Bobby Leon Poole."

In his white shirt and brown pants, Poole strode in with a stunned look on his face, as if he had no idea what was going on. *There he is,* I thought, *there's your monster.*

I sat back in the chair and stared at him as he placed his hand on the Bible, swearing to tell the truth.

At first, Phil was relaxed. He asked Poole basic questions about where he was incarcerated and what his charges were (he had pleaded guilty to six counts of first degree burglary, two counts of felonious larceny, rape, three counts of second-degree sex offense, and nine counts of misdemeanor breaking and entering), trying to get Poole to loosen up a bit. Then he started asking him about the statements he had made to Detective Gauldin at the time of his arrest.

"Did Detective Gauldin ask you questions about an incident that occurred at Brookwood Garden Condominiums?"

"That's the one I was arrested for," Poole shot back.

Phil asked him to recall the date—it was April, 21, 1985—and I scribbled it down in the legal pad I had in front of me. And then the judge cut Phil off.

"Mr. Moseley, deal first with some matter connected with this case."

I knew Phil had important questions he had to get in—he wanted to ask about the blood type of Bobby Poole.

"Mr. Poole, do you know what your blood type is?"

The judge was getting frustrated. "Mr. Moseley, deal with something more directly related to this case."

My blood type was O positive. The blood they found at the second crime scene was type A, same as Poole's. It seemed pretty directly related to me. There was no blood they could test from the first crime scene.

Phil switched directions, and then flat-out asked Poole, in an intimidating voice. "I ask you, Mr. Poole, did you go to Brookwood Garden Condominiums in the early morning hours of July 29, 1984, and unlawfully enter the condominium occupied by Jennifer Thompson?"

"No, sir."

"Did you enter her apartment and place your hand over—after being in her apartment for a time, place your hand over her mouth?"

"No, sir," he said.

"And then have oral intercourse with her and then vaginal intercourse?"

"No, sir."

"Did you rape her?"

"No, sir." He avoided eye contact with me, looking only at my attorney. I clenched my fists under the table. *Liar!*

Phil pushed on to the Mary Reynolds rape, firing the same kind of questions at him. Poole denied everything. He also denied going to Kenny for help with his case and denied that he confessed he had done the crimes I was incarcerated for. He kept responding, "No, sir," like he was completely puzzled as to why they were even asking him.

The lies rolled out of him easily. If anything bothered him, he didn't let on, except at one point while he was up on the stand, when Poole ran his hand over his chest and grimaced like he was having heartburn or some kind of chest pain. And when he did that, I noticed Ms. Reynolds flinch and bury her head in her husband's shoulder. *The grin.* Earlier, she had testified about the scary smile her rapist had made while grabbing at her through the window.

Then Mr. Turner started jumping in with objections, and Mr. Moseley told the judge that because it was a voir dire examination of the witness, he wanted the answers for the record.

"Mr. Moseley, unless you have some testimony to be elicited

from this witness pointing to the guilt of some third person, the court is not willing for you to put that in the record, and the motion to do so, even on voir dire, is denied."

Phil then tried to explain that they did have evidence Poole was the perpetrator, evidence that would come forward, including the fact that physically, Poole fit the description of the attacker given by both Mary and Jennifer, and he resembled the composite drawing. Then he started talking about the crimes Poole committed—after I was already shipped out to Central Prison—smashing porch lights and going in windows and back doors, sneaking up on women asleep in their beds or couches, that other women described him wearing white gloves or mittens, that he had several offenses on the same day. His MO, Phil said, was the same as that of the two rapes I was charged with.

The prosecutor, Turner, finally objected, and the judge sustained it. They were talking in circles, as far as I was concerned, about how the evidence only raised a suspicion that Poole was the perpetrator, and that the evidence was not "direct" enough for the jury to hear it. But what more did they have to connect *me* to this crime? If I testified, Phil warned me they'd say my prior juvenile record—breaking and entering with intent to commit second-degree rape—was "similar," even though what really happened was nothing like the crime committed upon these women. Why was that similar, but not Poole's crimes, which happened right around the time of these rapes I was being tried for? They said I looked like the composite, but to me, Poole looked more like the composite. The physical evidence was barely anything: a piece of foam they said came from my shoe, although I bet it could have come from almost anyone's sneaker; and a flashlight from my house—how many people had the same exact flashlight? When it came down to it, they had built a case against me simply because these two women said I did it. And since I'd messed up my alibi, who do you think they would believe?

But you had to hand it to Phil. He still stated all that information, himself, and the court reporter had to type it all up, even if the judge wouldn't let him get it in by questioning Poole.

Phil said he understood the court's ruling on the matter, but asked the judge to let him finish his point. Phil described more details from Poole's crimes and how similar they were to things that happened to Mary Reynolds and Jennifer Thompson, how he had pushed the pillow over someone's head like he was going to smother her, and how he left the panties on one leg, how he said in his statement to Gauldin that he used to walk around the Brookwood Gardens at three thirty in the morning, drunk and high from all the pot he had smoked. And finally he offered a lab report that showed Poole had an A blood type and was an A secretor, just like the spatter of blood found on the door frame of Mary Reynolds's apartment, which didn't belong to her or her husband. Or me, for that matter, because my blood type was O positive. Phil did a great job, in my mind, of showing that Poole had committed these crimes.

Poole was escorted out and the defense called Kenny. There was a long delay, since the bailiffs had to make sure they didn't cross paths.

Kenny told the court that he was afraid of testifying, but he did it. He told Phil about Poole's confession. The prosecutor seemed to enjoy questioning Kenny, like he was having a conversation with everyone in the courtroom: *Why would we ever believe a word a convicted felon had to say?* They may say "justice for all" and "innocent until proven guilty," but it just doesn't play that way in court.

At the end of the voir dire examination, the judge didn't think any of this evidence pointed directly to Poole and ruled that it be excluded. That meant members of the jury would have no idea that Bobby Leon Poole existed, or that he had committed a bunch of crimes virtually identical to the ones I was accused of—even at the exact apartment complex, and had bragged in prison about getting away with it. The voir dire thing just felt unfair; I mean, if they were so sure it was me, why couldn't the jury hear everything and decide for themselves? The truth mattered less than getting me convicted, I guess. When the judge hit his gavel, he might as well have been hammering another nail into my coffin.

So the jury marched back on in, and Jennifer Thompson took the stand.

"Who was the person that raped you on the twenty-ninth of July 1984, Ms. Thompson?" Mr. Turner asked.

She confidently said, "Ronald Junior Cotton."

Mr. Turner said, "Is Mr. Cotton in the courtroom today, and would you point him out please?"

"He's right there," she said, pointing at me like this whole thing was a waste of time. I couldn't believe it. Poole had been right there in the courtroom, and neither one of the women recognized him.

. . .

The trial went on, with many of the same people from the first trial testifying again. My old boss from Somer's Seafood, Mr. Byrum, took the stand. I'd never had any problems with him. Ray Byrum was a full-blooded Native American; he had a head full of curly black hair, and was heavyset with a potbelly that arrived about a minute before the rest of him did. He was all cleaned up, like he was dressed for church on a Sunday. As a matter of fact, sometimes the court seemed as quiet as a church, just about the exact opposite of the noise in the penitentiary. For the DA, Byrum was a witness to say he had seen me wearing white gloves when I rode my bike, which I did. It kept my hands from getting dirty. Only I used to cut all the fingers off them. They were leather.

Then Turner began to ask some strange questions.

"During the time Mr. Cotton was in your employ, did you have the occasion to personally witness any problems with Mr. Cotton, while he was working for you?"

"Well, the one problem was with the waitresses, it wasn't with doing his job."

Mr. Turner looked very concerned when he asked what that problem was. Ray said I was always "messing with them."

"How do you mean, 'messing with them,' Mr. Byrum?"

"Touching them, on their shoulders, and their bodies, and their rears, and telling dirty jokes."

I could see members of the jury looking at me, disgusted. I probably flirted here or there, but it wasn't like what he was saying. I suspected that someone coached him to say this, maybe one of the cops paid him a visit. Dan dropped his head and let out a big sigh. Phil objected. Ray told them I did this every time I worked. Then the prosecutor asked how old the waitresses were. Ray said there were two I bothered most. "One was, like, eighteen; and one was forty-seven, I believe."

And then Mr. Turner asked, "What was the race of these wait-resses?"

"White," Ray answered.

. . .

For eight days, I sat there silently while the State made me sound like a predator, while Jennifer Thompson and Mary Reynolds pointed their fingers at me and called me a rapist. During the closing arguments, although I tried to concentrate, my mind drifted as I kept asking myself, How had I gotten here?

When I was young, I wanted to be a police officer. I watched *Starsky and Hutch, Hawaii Five-O,* all those cop shows where they were heroes. In the end, they always came to the rescue, stopping the bad guy from hurting people. I wanted to be a hero like that.

The first time I ever got in trouble, I knew that dream was history. I was in third grade, and I always wanted to tag along with my older brother Calvin, who was about twelve. Calvin knew the Green brothers, Stevie and Paulie, who were probably fourteen and fifteen. The Greens washed dishes at a little doughnut place across the railroad tracks from our house in Glen Raven. My brother Calvin used to bust them about these silly paper hats they had to wear.

Paulie, who everyone called Hops, told us the Donut Shop left money in the cash register overnight. "I'll leave the back door un-locked," he said.

The next night, Calvin and I rode our bikes and parked them in the lot of Hewitt's BBQ next door. We walked around the back and through the unlocked door. Hops was already there, passing out the cash. I stuffed some in my pocket. I knew it was wrong, but since we weren't beating anybody up or kicking a door in, it didn't seem as if I was committing some big crime. We walked back out the door and were headed back to our bikes with Calvin taunting me saying, "I got more money than you-ou, I got more money than you-ou," when the owners Ricky and Harry came out of nowhere. I guess the Green brothers didn't know about the silent alarm.

"Y'all hold up right there," Harry said, pointing a shotgun at us.

They marched us back inside the Donut Shop, and the four of us sat in a booth waiting for the Alamance County sheriff.

When he showed up, he took us down to the station and we got court dates. The sheriff drove us back to the BBQ parking lot, and said he was going to follow us home. He rolled slowly behind us in his cruiser while Calvin and I pedaled on our bikes, our legs shaking. When my father arrived, he made me go into the yard and pick some switches off a tree or a bush. "Get another one," he said, when I handed him a couple. He tied three sticks together and grabbed me by my wrist, although I tried to run a circle around him as he hit me.

"It's Calvin's fault! He told me to do it!" I pleaded.

"Well, you can't always listen to your older brother, 'cause he ain't always right. If you were wrong, you were wrong," he said, and made me swear I'd keep out of trouble.

Looking back, that was just the beginning. I had a probation officer come to check on me in elementary school. I was the bad guy already, at nine years old. I would never be a hero. So I continued making stupid mistakes, never thinking about the consequences. There again in the courtroom, I was on the wrong side of the law, and no one believed a word I said. I was the bad guy; it was that simple to them. I knew the trial had not gone well.

Before the court broke for lunch, I said to Phil, "How's it looking?"

I knew the answer already, but I hoped Phil or Dan might tell me something else, give me some reason to hope as I headed back to jail to eat lunch.

"I don't know, Ron, it's looking pretty difficult here." He put his hand on my shoulder. "We'll see what the jury believes and doesn't believe."

. . .

While I was eating, another inmate, a baby-faced bald guy with a goatee asked me how things were going.

"They're sending me down the river on a boat with no paddles. I'm being railroaded."

We kept talking for a few minutes. I told him about the crimes, that I was innocent. He asked me my name. His was Duncan.

" 'Cotton'? Man, I heard about you! My buddy Dennis was just talking about you, said you were in court today. He was going on about how he knew you were innocent. He said a coupla years ago, he was in here with a guy named Poole, and Poole told him he did those crimes."

I stopped eating and stared at him. "What? What guy?"

"Bass. Dennis Bass. He's here, man. Ask him yourself."

Instead, I told Phil about it and, early the next morning, before we went over to the court, Phil and Dan talked to Bass and Duncan, themselves. It was our last shot. As the final day of the trial began, Phil and Dan immediately made a motion for the court to reopen the evidence, or declare a mistrial. Then they approached the bench and whispered to the judge. The judge denied the motions, and submitted all the evidence—none of it mentioning Poole—to the jury so they could begin deliberations.

Phil and Dan told me they would get a sworn affidavit from Bass to include in the papers should they need to file an appeal. The jury filed out of the room at about ten in the morning, and I stayed in a little holding room off the courtroom.

It took just about an hour for the jury to decide, and I watched the jury foreman hand over a piece of paper that was the key to the rest of my life. I held my breath as the clerk stood up to read.

"Members of the jury, your foreman has returned as your verdict that the defendant Ronald Junior Cotton is guilty of first-degree burglary of the dwelling of Jennifer Thompson. Is this your verdict? If so, raise your right hand, please." Every single one of them raised their hands.

My head went somewhere else as the clerk continued to read "guilty" for the rest of the five charges. *Guilty. Guilty. Guilty. Guilty. Guilty.* The words spun like a tire stuck in mud, over and over. The prosecutor looked up, blinking back tears, as if heaven had answered his prayers. Tears of victory for sending an innocent black man to prison, while I was the one that should have wept. But I was beyond words, or tears.

As in the trial before, the judge asked me if I would like to say anything. "Mr. Cotton, if you desire to speak as to what you think the court ought to do with you, in light of the jury's verdict and the law, you may speak, and whatever you say will be taken into account in passing judgment. You're not obliged to speak, but if you wish to, I'll hear and consider anything you wish to say."

Phil and Dan raised their eyebrows at me, but there was nothing left to lose. For three years, the words I'd said added up to nothing. All the letters I had written, all the words Phil and Dan argued for me, and nothing. The only words people heard were "guilty" and "rapist." The decisions about my life were no longer in my hands, but I wanted people to know that regardless of the outcome, it wasn't going to knock me down. They could judge me by my past, but they didn't know me at all. So I decided to express myself in the only way I knew how.

My wooden chair made noise as I pushed it back and stood up. "Yes, sir, your honor. I'd just like to stay and say—you know, I've been found guilty by the jury here today for crimes I never committed. I sympathize with Ms. Reynolds, Ms. Thompson, I mean, even though I never saw them a day in my life until the incident had taken place and I was taken into custody at the police department. And I would ask that you take into consideration all of these offenses that took place and the time that I would get from these sentences, if you would, run them in concurrent.

"I just have something that I'd like to leave among the hearts of each and every one of you in this courtroom here today. It's more of a little song, and if I may have an opportunity to say a few brief words from that song that was written by me in the county jail. If that's OK with you. May I?"

The judge just stared at me for a minute, like he wasn't sure what I was trying to pull, before saying, "Yes, sir."

There seemed to be no other sound in the courtroom. My family sat directly behind me, so I could not see them. What I saw was a cold wall of faces—the judge, the jury, the DA—who looked at me like I was something to be despised, something less than human.

I cleared my throat, and I sang.

Decisions I can no longer make,
Because my future is so unknown to me,
And that I could no longer take,
'Cause during the day I wonder,
at night I hurt with fear
Call out your name so much
'Til suddenly tears appear
. . . until God came in my life,
Until God came in my life.

I was often alone,
People I really couldn't face,
I just didn't know what to do,
Without God I felt so out of place,
And if only you could see me,
Then you would know how I feel.
I'm not the same person I used to be;
Sometimes I don't think that this is real.
How many times must I say this
Before you agree
There's no other God could ever love you,
quite as much as Lord God
Believe me, God will change your life
And that is a fact,
Because I would pray
Both night and day,
Until God came into my life.

When I finished, I looked again at those faces. Some were angry, I guess, because I didn't show remorse. How can you be sorry for something you didn't do? Other people looked at each other as if to say, *He's facing two life sentences plus one hundred and eighty years, and he's singing? What's wrong with him?* Phil and Dan had bowed their heads, like, if they looked up, the bailiff would have come over and clobbered them with his flashlight.

CHAPTER 9

"MAN, I CAN'T BELIEVE YOU go for a new trial and come back with more time than you left," Roger Blackstock, the prison's legal eagle, said to me when I got back to Raleigh, just in time for the "special" Thanksgiving meal of turkey and gravy. He looked at some of my papers concerning the second charge. "They done you wrong, Cotton. Your lawyer going to appeal this?"

I nodded. Usually when you get "called out" to go back to court after being in prison, at the very least you come back with a reduced sentence. But not in my case. In the end, I was convicted of two counts of first-degree burglary, first-degree rape, first-degree sexual offense, second-degree rape, and second-degree sexual offense, and sentenced to two life sentences plus fifty-four years. The only stroke of luck—if you could even call it that—was that the judge agreed to let the two life sentences run concurrently.

Returning to Central Prison could have crushed me. If I had

let myself think freedom was coming only to have it taken away again, I'm sure I would have wound up like the men so medicated they wandered around like zombies, hopped up on Thorazine. It didn't take much to spot them in the yard: It would be ninety degrees out and they'd have all of their clothes on at once. Long shirts piled on top of each other. The prison got inside their heads, and once it does that, you're gone. That's what it means when people say, "The time is doing you."

The way pipes burst when there's too much pressure—I couldn't allow that pressure to build up in me, because it'd snap my mind. I had to protect my mind, to get in front of the time. The first four years of Central Prison had been pure survival, a constant fight against the reality of my situation. Now it was time for me to make peace with the fact that I might not ever get out. Phil wrote to tell me there was nothing more he could do for me after the second trial. My case would be referred to the North Carolina Appellate Defender's Office, and they'd handle the appeal. "We'll help them the best we can," Phil wrote.

More waiting, carrying a big question mark over my head. If this was my life—if I was going to spend the rest of my days in a North Carolina prison—I had to figure out a way to live it.

. . .

Coming back to Central Prison was easier because Poole was gone, and so was Kenny. Kenny must've been transferred while I was awaiting trial in Graham. I did anything I could to keep busy while I awaited word of my appeal. I could draw a rose well enough, and guys paid me ten or fifteen cents to draw a flower or something on the envelopes they were sending their letters in. I also went back to work in the kitchen. But now it was time to hustle.

In my dorm, I became friendly with a couple of guys who bunked near me. David slept on the bunk above me, and Randy was to the side of us. They both worked in the sign shop, making license tags. David had to be around fifty-something and was balding, with brownish-blond hair. A short guy with a hump on his back, he had been incarcerated for almost twenty-five years already and was always trying to figure out how to make another dollar . . . when he wasn't high. David had been in a medium-security facility but got caught trying to escape, so that's why he was back at Central. Randy was in his thirties, and had a cowboy-style mustache, biggish ears, and eyes that always looked like he was only half-awake. He was a big pothead, too.

"Cotton, we got a business proposition for ya," Randy said one day in the dorm. He motioned for me to come over to talk to him and David.

"We were discussing starting a little business—making and selling buck. We need someone inside the kitchen for the supplies."

I nodded. "Buck" was homemade wine. As with any kind of alcohol you got your hands on in society, when you drank it, you thought you could really do something. You were the best lover or the best fighter, and you'd buck up at people, starting fights. Once I saw a guy drunk on buck wail on a child molester who had been sitting reading the Bible, minding his own business. This guy took a belt with a padlock on the end of it and pounded the child molester in the head and face. "*What did I do? What did I do?"* the child molester cried. I'm sure the guy who was beating him would have killed him if COs hadn't stopped him first.

"The split'll be three way," David said.

"What do y'all need?" I said.

David told me to get yeast, sugar, and anything I could find to flavor the wine: potatoes, tomato paste, grapes, orange juice, or rice. Then we made a plan for how I'd get the stuff to them. We worked out when they would come into the chow hall to eat while I was on the job in the kitchen, and I knew what side they planned to eat on. Whatever I could find that day from the list of ingredients, I'd wrap in cellophane. When they finished eating and brought their steel trays to the washing area, I'd meet them. In the space between the Plexiglas and the counter where a used tray was pushed across to the guy who washed them, I'd pass out a package. David or Randy would take it, slide his shirt up and slip the package into the waistband of his pants, and walk out. On my own, I would smuggle out some of the large plastic bags the milk came in, after having rinsed them out with hot water.

After we got everything we needed, we gathered together in the dorm. Randy or I would keep a lookout for an officer while David made the wine. If a corrections officer headed our way, we'd yell, "Man down!" and scramble to hide everything.

In the plastic milk bags, we'd mix whatever I'd been able to get that week—potatoes or tomato paste—then the sugar, then the yeast, and finally water. We'd shake the bag real good. At first we put it in our pillowcases for about four days, letting it cook. To disguise the smell from officers coming around to do check, we'd smear BENGAY around or place an old can with soapy slivers under the bunk. Then we figured we could use the heat vent in the cell to speed up the process, so we pulled off the vent cover and placed the bag inside, then put the cover back. Sometimes the buck was ready the next day.

Before we put it out on the market, we had to test it. It was always kind of a gamble trying to figure out how to balance the yeast and the sugar. If you didn't do it right, you'd end up with vinegar that nobody would want. I remember sitting there playing cards with Randy and David, sipping buck and getting drunk. David had the biggest grin on his face; he was always the man with the plan. When we had a good batch, we bought coffee cups at the canteen and opened for business. A cup was a dollar, and a pitcher—an empty hot water bottle, if you had one—went for three dollars. We made sure we had buck prepared for the two paydays: Wednesdays, when they deposited your earnings from your prison job into your inmate trust fund, and Fridays, when you could withdraw again.

A few years later, I found out David ended up getting killed trying to escape from Salisbury, another prison. He had jumped the fence, and was running toward the second one when a CO shot him in the head. I picture him, in those few seconds in between the fences, a stoner grin on his face, high at the thought that freedom was so close.

• • •

Bars or not, I had to make something of myself, something more than forty cents a day in the kitchen. My family did what they could far as sending me money from time to time, but I felt bad taking their hard-earned cash. With my profit from the buck, I began to stockpile items from Central's canteen and started my own business running a canteen. I did my business at night, after the prison's canteen had closed for the day. You wanted chips at 9:00 P.M.? I had them. I marked things up, usually between twenty-five and thirty cents. When I had a lot of inventory, I brought in people to work for me, letting them eat what they wanted for free in exchange for keeping chips or cans of soup in their lockers for me. Eventually I got a reputation for wheeling and dealing.

· · ·

Despite what happened at the last trial, my sister Diane continued to believe that God had spoken to her, and she wrote me often.

> We've had a hard life, and we still don't have much. But I'm free in my heart, I'm happy in my heart. The Lord knows how much we can bear. He knows the outcome of your life before you got into this situation. There is a reason, Ron. Be free in your heart.

That was easy for her to say, of course, because she wasn't sitting in some prison. The closest thing I felt to freedom were the small bursts of joy I had singing. I looked forward to getting back to the choir at Central, having missed singing with the guys all those months I had been in Alamance County jail for the trial. Long after practice ended, the words echoed in my head like another prayer.

> *What a fellowship, what a joy divine,*
> *leaning on the everlasting arms;*
> *what a blessedness, what a peace is mine,*
> *leaning on the everlasting arms.*

• • •

In June, I was transferred to a medium-security facility, a farm in Halifax County. It might sound good on paper—going from maximum to medium security, but I think the prison system did it on purpose, shifting people around like gears in a car so you couldn't get too comfortable. And that's exactly what I was. I didn't want to call Central Prison "home," but I had lived there for four years; I had fought my battles to earn my spot. I didn't want to give up my corner bunk. But I had no choice. Early one morning, COs came to get me and, before I knew it, I was at Sandy Ridge transfer terminal, boarding a Grey Goose filled with other inmates with a sign reading "Caledonia"—the same prison Bobby Poole transferred to over a year ago.

Caledonia had two components to it: the farm and the huge cannery where all the produce was packaged. I got a job in the cannery. Other inmates picked tomatoes, sweet potatoes, collard greens, and put them on an assembly line, where they were canned, labeled, and thrown down a little chute. That's where I came in. I'd box the cans and send them off to be wrapped and shipped to prisons, schools, and hospitals all over the state. I probably made over a thousand boxes a day, putting six cans in a case and stacking fifteen cases on a skid.

There was no choir at Caledonia, so I stopped singing and went back to the punching bag. Working out there one day, I felt someone looking at me. Prison really makes you grow eyes on the back of your head. I looked back, and there was Bobby Leon Poole, staring at me with his cold eyes. I stared back until he moved off. I turned back to the bag and pounded it.

"Cotton, your hands are bleeding," a guy said to me when I returned to the dorm.

"I know."

For now, it was better than taking it out on another inmate.

I rinsed my hands and let the blood dry, then I lay on my bed and wrote my appellate defender a letter.

July 9, 1988

Dear Sir:

I'm writing to let you know that I'm no longer an inmate at Central Prison. I was recommended for medium custody and transferred to the Tillery prison unit. So if you have information concerning my case, I'd appreciate it if you send it to my new location.

The unit I'm on now has really put me a great distance from home to where it would be extremely difficult for my family or friends to pay me a visit. Plus, Bobby Leon Poole is on this unit and I really care not to have him within my view, knowing that I'm serving the time in prison for crimes he committed.

I'm not afraid of this Poole guy, but what I am afraid of is having the two of us in the same unit. I feel that something serious might take place between the two of us and I know deep in my heart that I wouldn't want anything like that to take place. So what I'm asking you to do is see if you can get me back to Central Prison or at least to another unit.

Respectfully submitted,
Ronald Cotton

•   •   •

Poole would turn out to be the least of my worries. He was housed on another unit, so I didn't have much contact with him.

"Medium custody" meant you were in an open dormitory, whereas in close custody, you were in a cell. In many ways, being in a cell was a lot safer than being out in an open dorm. Trouble was never hard to find in prison.

One night, while I sat out where the TV was to watch the news, this guy Donnie came in, looking like someone had pissed in his cornflakes.

"What you doing sitting in my seat?" he yelled.

"I don't see your fucking name on it," I replied.

It was always important to show you weren't weak, that you couldn't be taken advantage of. Fighting back, even when you lost, earned you respect. Donnie walked out. But I knew it was on.

A few days later, I was playing cards with another guy when someone came over and tapped me on the shoulder. I turned and *bam!* Donnie popped me in the face. I dove forward, grabbing him around the waist, and threw him over my head onto the bunks. He jumped off and straight onto me, wrapping his legs around my waist and choking me. I took off running toward the bars, hoping I'd knock him out by slamming him into them, but he hung on, squeezing my neck so hard I thought I was going to black out. So I took hold of his testicles.

"Let go," I wheezed.

"Let go of my balls!" he shouted at me, some of the spit in the corners of his mouth landing on my face.

I fell forward across a bunk, hoping to bang his head against the metal edge of it. But I judged it wrong, and the bunk above hit me in the head. I was close to blacking out again when I heard another inmate start whistling—letting Donnie know the COs were on their way.

"Motherfucker, it ain't over," he said, getting off me as I gasped for air.

. . .

Working at the cannery, I got to know a guy named Ricky Sutcliffe, who had curly brown hair and thick glasses. He was serving time for the same charges—first-degree sexual offense, first-degree rape, first-degree breaking and entering—and, like me, he said he was an innocent man. I don't know if he was or wasn't. It was hard to believe anything anyone said. A lot of people in prison say they're innocent. Others lie about their charges. Most people, for security reasons, say they're in for murder. It makes them seem badass, I guess. One guy told me he had come home to find his wife in bed with another man, so he killed them both. Only later did I find out that he raped an eight-year-old girl. Some of the nicest people you met in prison were sometimes the ones who had done the worst stuff. You just never knew who to believe. Some people told lies because they didn't want to accept what they had done. A couple of times I tried to tell people I didn't do it, but they usually just said, "You had to, if you didn't do it, you wouldn't be here."

Ricky had a bad habit of borrowing money from the loan sharks in prison, so he went in and out of protective custody. Somebody always seemed to be after him. One day, I was out in the yard and spotted a wrench stuck between the fence, and I told Ricky about it later when I went to work.

"You think you could get it to me?" Ricky asked. "They said if I didn't pay soon, I had two choices: blood on a shank or shit on a dick."

I knew Ricky was having a lot of trouble, and ad seg wasn't going to help him much. If you checked off—filled out a form requesting administrative segregation for yourself—word spread and they'd just come after you when you got out. Eventually, you had to pay in prison, one way or another.

"Yeah, man, I can help you out," I said. There was a boiler room near the area I had spotted the wrench, so I had him plan to meet me later in the yard so I could toss it over the fence to him just before I went inside. Later on, guards caught him with it and asked him where he got it from and he sold me out. I did six days in the hole for that. It pissed me off, and Ricky thought I wanted to hurt him. He cowered when he saw me, but I told him he already had enough trouble to worry about.

The hole was a ten-by-eight-foot cell with a bunk, commode, and small sink. Some guys couldn't take being in there. They'd holler and scream, urinate and defecate into cups to toss on the officers when they walked by; others cut themselves. I tried to look at it as a room to go into to rest: It was a break from the population, where I could catch up on correspondence without always having to look over my shoulder. To keep myself in shape, I filled trash bags with water and lifted them like the weights I used in the rec room, and did sit-ups and push-ups. And I prayed. I prayed that seeing me again shook up Bobby Poole, that his conscience would gnaw at him, and that he'd eventually confess.

Soon after I got out of lockup, Ricky transferred out to Odom Farm. The COs must have known enough about the contract on his head. A couple of months later, I spotted his cousin in the chow hall.

"What's up?" I nodded at him.

"You hear about Ricky? He hung himself. Stupid bastard," he said sadly.

It shocked me, knowing he went out like that after all the months we worked together packing cans. Here one minute, gone the next. It probably sounds crazy, but it made me feel like my problems weren't that big. Death or escape were not my only options. I still had a chance at an appeal, and I believed that the Lord had his reasons for me being in this situation. Sometimes, all I had to cling to was the personal knowledge that I was innocent, and even if no one else knew that, God did. It made me feel more connected to him.

· · ·

My family tried to visit when they could, but it was harder for them to get down to Halifax. Still, they sent letters and money when they were able to. There were a few months where I didn't hear from Diane, and then I got a letter that explained why. She had been dating Tim, a guy she said looked and sounded just like Luther Vandross. But four months in, she found out Tim was a big liar. He was running coke and other drugs, and he was married. So one night they met at a hotel, and Diane tried to end it. Tim wouldn't accept her answer. He took out his gun and told her he didn't want to live without her. Diane thought he was going to kill her, but instead he shot himself in the head. He just slumped over, right on the bed, blood everywhere, and Diane ran out into the parking lot, screaming her head off. The police tried to say Diane did it, until they checked her hands for gunpowder and realized there was no way she could have been holding the gun. Someone told her, "You might as well leave town, because they got it in for the Cottons."

Once again, I could not be with my family when they needed me. I wanted to believe God had a plan, but I wondered if I would ever be anything other than a burden on my family. I prayed to God to give me the strength to endure, to keep me out of trouble with the other inmates. Much as I tried to keep to myself and release my tension on the punching bag, I didn't have control over what other inmates might do—especially the ones that were never going home. Put a man in a cage with beasts and throw away the key, and it's usually not very long before the man is a beast himself. I knew my innocence would not matter if I gave in to the violence all around me.

. . .

One morning, I woke up and got my things from my locker and was getting ready to head out to the yard, when Donnie appeared between the bunks, blocking my way.

He looked completely crazy, like he just slithered out of some womb: shirt off, hair slicked back, and all over his bare chest, arms, neck, and face, he had smeared petroleum jelly. I'd have a hard time getting a grip on him. And it only took me a fraction of a second to spot the shoestring tied around his waist with a shank hanging from it.

"Red motherfucker!" he spat.

I thought this really might be it. Five years, two trials, and I would die there between the bunks, never able to clear my name. But maybe God was looking out for me. Because another inmate sleeping nearby woke up and yelled, "Shut up!" and then some COs came in to see what all the commotion was. They hauled off Donnie to lockup.

My days in medium custody out in the open dorms soon came to an end. I let a guy borrow my sneakers to play basketball. He put them back under my bunk when he was finished, and I forgot about it. But a few days later while I was out in the yard, I got called into the office.

"These your shoes?" they asked.

"Yeah."

They pulled a homemade shank out of one of them.

"That's not mine," I said.

The officers didn't buy it and I was busted back to close custody. In close custody, I had a lot less freedom to move around, and I got assigned field detail. Summer or winter, rain or shine, inmates were loaded up on the work bus and driven for ten or fifteen minutes to the farms, where they picked vegetables while armed guards on horseback kept an eye on them. In the end, staying in close custody—in a cell instead of exposed in the open dorms—probably kept me alive.

. . .

After I was convicted for the second time, they appointed a guy from the appellate defender's office to handle my appeal to the North Carolina Court of Appeals. I didn't hear from him regularly, and I later learned that he had not raised the best argument available to me: that the judge had committed something called "reversible error" by keeping the Poole evidence from the jury. I felt screwed. Of course, the North Carolina Court of Appeals upheld the conviction in August 1990. Later, a man named Malcolm Hunter, Jr. from the appellate defender's office delivered the news. Because of "family reasons" with the first guy, Mr. Hunter said he was taking over my case, and that I still had another chance at the Supreme Court of North Carolina.

It sank me fast. Much as I tried to prepare myself, I knew I was running out of options.

August 8, 1990

Dear Mr. Hunter, Jr.,
I received your sad mail today. It broke my heart to know that I was denied a new trial knowing I'm an innocent man. I wish I was dead. I thought about doing something I know later down the road I would regret. I accept this losing battle knowing I still have a chance in Supreme Court. . . .

Twenty days later, I received his reply, in which he wrote, "Do not lose heart, Mr. Cotton. We have not finished your case by a long shot."

• • •

In close custody, the single cells all faced the yard. Narrow windows gave us some natural light, but they were supposed to be sealed shut. A lot of us, though, figured out how to remove the sealing in the frame, so you could move the window up a little and get some fresh air. One day, when I was walking to the basketball court, a guy called to me from his window.

"Cotton, c'mere a minute. You want a cat?"

I stepped closer, and he passed me out a tiny calico kitten who had to be less than a month old. She had a tan spot between her eyes. I had a jacket on, so I put her down my sleeve, resting on my forearm. I took her back to my cell and put her on the floor, then I went to the canteen and purchased milk and sardines.

When I opened the tin, she squeaked a meow and buried her head in them. Then she lapped up the milk. After she got her fill, she hopped up on the bunk and crawled up on me, resting her head on my shoulder. I decided to call her Judy.

When I'd get up in the morning, I had to make sure Judy was fed, and put clean newspaper on the floor. After I showered in the evenings, she was usually there, waiting for me on my bunk. Although she liked her sardines and milk, Judy was still a little wild. She liked to come and go as she pleased, so I fixed my window to leave it up. I learned what she was trying to say: if her milk went bad, she'd hop up on the back of my commode and stare down at the water. And sometimes, she'd come looking for me, running out in the yard through the population, trying to spot my shoes.

Judy got in a few scuffles with some of the other animals: once she came back with a big scratch over her eye, and when she was about a year old, she had kittens herself. Someone told me they had spotted her on the work bus, nursing about four kittens. Then she moved them to a trash can near the facility. I went out and retrieved them, carrying the babies, with their eyes still closed up, to my cell. That night, Judy came in and brought the kittens back outside, one by one, and placed them in a ditch near the work bus. For some reason, she just didn't want her babies inside. But there was a rainstorm and the ditch flooded, drowning all the kittens.

They moved me from a cell on the ground floor to the second floor, so I packed my belongings in a shopping bag and put her inside. "Stay down," I told her. But as I passed the guard station, she must have heard their voices and decided to investigate. Out popped her little head.

"Cotton, you got to let that cat go," the CO said.

So I took her out in the yard and put her down.

I went up to my cell and looked out the window. Judy stood down in the yard, meowing. I got to work, taking off the window seal, and then shoved my blanket out through it.

"Jump, Judy! Jump!" I called out.

She hurled herself at it and dug in her claws so I could raise her up. And after that, when she wanted out, I'd put her on the blanket and lower her out until she could jump off.

• • •

In 1991, the Supreme Court of North Carolina upheld my convictions. I read Mr. Hunter's letter and put it down on my chest. Judy hopped up, demanding I scratch her around the ears. "Looks like you're stuck with me," I told her.

DOC officials informed me I was being shipped out again, this time to Southern Correctional Institution in Troy. A few weeks before the transfer, Judy disappeared. I had heard there were a couple of guys who were hurting the animals, slicing their tongues out, and I put the word out that if I found out someone did something to my cat, I'd kill him. But nothing ever came back to me, including Judy. I told myself Judy knew she didn't really belong here and somehow wiggled out under one of the fences, and maybe some young girl found her and took her in. That's how I pictured her, getting fat on some nice family's couch, with nothing to worry about.

. . .

Tudy and my father drove down to visit me once in Troy. They had gotten very lost, they said. Diane was supposed to come with them, but Tudy said her nerves were still shot. She had gone on disability after her boyfriend had committed suicide in front of her, and lived with my mother, taking care of her. We sat across from each other at a table—Troy being one of the prisons where you could have contact with your family, hug them, and take pictures.

"Happy birthday, Ron," Tudy said. She had made me some cookies, and gave me a card filled with money she had collected from the family. I had turned thirty a few months before. Looking at her and my father, I thought we all looked older.

"How you holding up, son?" my father asked. He looked like an old man, his hand resting on top of a cane. Hell, eight years had passed, and he *was* an old man.

"The lawyer, Hunter, he says it's not over yet, but I don't know. I'm getting tired. Sometimes I think it would be easier to just let go and accept my situation."

"We're still praying for you," Tudy said. "Somehow, some way, you're going to be free one day."

"Toot, the Supreme Court denied the appeal—"

"Poole's got to confess one of these days. What man would want that mark on his soul?" my father said.

I shrugged. "He didn't seem to mind lying in court."

"Look son, my health's not good. There's gonna come a time where I can't travel the distance to visit you anymore. I'll still write you, and send you what I can. Justice will prevail. I know in my heart that God will see to it that justice is done," my father said.

"But there's nothing left after the Supreme Court. The lawyers said there wasn't anything to take it up to the federal court. That door is closed."

"Then you're going to have to wait for one to open," he said.

"Or find the window," Tudy said, laughing. It lifted my heart up to hear her laugh.

When you moved between units in prison—or went from the visiting area to the dorms—you'd go through sally ports. You'd walk through a door into a sealed kind of hallway, and the door would close behind you and lock. Someone would be watching on a camera or from a booth nearby, and you had to wait before they opened the next door in front of you. This was how they controlled the population flow; in case of a riot, it was also how they'd seal the doors off.

Outside the visitation area, I stepped into the sally port, hearing the buzz that signaled the door behind me had closed. I waited, just like my father said, for another door to open.

CHAPTER 10

EARLY IN SEPTEMBER 1992, Mr. Hunter wrote me to say that an attorney and law professor named Richard Rosen had agreed to look into my case to see if anything could be done to help me. Mr. Hunter wanted to know if I was interested in his help. After so many doors had been slammed shut, I jumped at the chance for someone to find a way to crack open one of them and shine light on the truth. I wrote him back immediately.

Sept. 9, 1992

Mr. Hunter, Jr:

Sir, yes, I'd really appreciate the assistance of Mr. Rosen, and I want to thank you for doing what you could to help me. I really do! I feel if I don't get any help from the court system, I might as well call this place home.

I have been incarcerated eight years now for crimes I know I never committed, and God is my witness. I hurt daily and find it difficult to accept what I'm now having to go through. No one understands and it seems no one cares. I've been fighting this battle a very long time, and my mind and heart have been left with a trademark that I'll never be able to overcome.

There have been times that I wish I was never born, because the life in which I now live is nothing but pure hurt. I'd rather be dead and in hell than to have to spend the rest of my entire life wasting away here.

I've done things that I'm not too proud of myself, but I don't deserve this, sir.

Sincerely,
Ronald Cotton

. . .

Richard Rosen was a full-time professor at UNC–Chapel Hill, home of my favorite basketball team, the Tar Heels. He was a very busy man, but he wrote me right away, and soon after sent a student down to interview me. They said they were going through all the transcripts from the trials.

October 4, 1992

Dear Mr. Rosen:

I received your letter and was pleased to learn that you are willing to assist me in my tragic situation. By all means, God bless you and I wish you the very best of luck. I'm hoping and praying that you're able to open some doors in this matter.

Mr. Rosen, allow me to say I'm an innocent man and there is no doubt I was indeed framed basically from my past record and my interracial relationship that I was involved in at the time of the crimes I was accused and convicted of. God is my witness. Sir, I honestly feel without a doubt that the people involved that caused me to get falsely convicted know that I'm innocent but just wanted me off the streets, and they've done a pretty good job of it, wouldn't you say?

I've been incarcerated since August 1, 1984, and living my life in the system has been extremely difficult knowing I'm innocent, waking up every day as I do these last eight years knowing I'm serving time for another man's crime. It's not easy and it's been rough for my family as well, especially my poor mother and father. My father lives in Orange County and if you need to get in touch with him you may at this address: P.O. Box [redacted], Hillsborough, N.C. 27278, phone 919-[redacted]-0438 or 4038. I've just forgotten my own father's phone no., this place really has me mixed up but I'm going to make it one way or the other.

I haven't heard anything other concerning Bobby Leon Poole because he's at Caledonia, Odom Complex located in Halifax County. I did learn he was telling people he was in for armed robbery and how he once stalked women out late at night and raped them. That man, Poole, I feel without a doubt has me doing his time and I'm willing to submit to any test that's available to prove to the courts I'm not guilty.

Sincerely,
Ronald Cotton

• • •

That fall, I met Mr. Rosen in person. Immediately, he told me to call him Rich. Even though he wasn't as formal as Phil—he didn't wear suits much and his shirt was never tucked in—he looked very much in control. He was a slim, trim guy with a bad back and his hair was going gray, it seemed to me, from wisdom of being in the law for so long. He told me he was going to ask a Burlington attorney, a former student of his named Tom

Lambeth, to help out with the case. Tom was local, Rich explained; he had grown up in Burlington, so he knew all the players in the community. I thought bringing in Tom sounded like a good idea.

Before he left, Rich said, "I can't promise you anything, but we'll do our best."

Their plan was to reinvestigate the case from the beginning. I really felt that they were going to do everything they could to achieve true justice—not because they were getting paid, either. I was considered "indigent"—my family didn't have the money to pay for a private attorney—so Rich stood to gain nothing from all the work he was doing. No one forced him to take this on. Rich said he and Tom had met with Phil and Dan, who turned over all the files from my case.

Rich kept me very well informed of what was going on throughout the rest of the year. It was more contact than I ever had with any lawyer since I had been incarcerated, and it really helped me feel that things were moving in my case, that it wasn't just sitting like still water.

In early November, I spoke with my father by phone. He told me he'd be willing to do what the good Lord allowed him to do, money-wise, to help out the lawyers with their investigation. I knew sometimes the State had the money to hire private investigators, but if you were like me, from a poor family, you were stuck with the lawyer the court assigned to you. More often than not, the court-appointed attorneys didn't care a bit about you. They weren't getting their regular rate, and they didn't have the budget to do a lot of investigating. If you want to call anything about my situation "lucky," though, at least I had Phil Moseley. I had to give Phil credit for still caring after we lost the second trial, when he didn't owe me anything. But I guess the blood evidence really shook him—later he told me it was a "one-o'clock-in-the-morning revelation," finding that the spot of blood on Ms. Reynolds's door frame matched Poole's blood type, not mine—stuff the jury and the appeals court wouldn't know. My letters could have just gone into his heartbreak pile, but Rich told me Phil wrote the appellate defender's office when he found out they had not raised important issues on the appeal. I guess that first guy had just done a rush job, and Mr. Hunter felt bad about it. Without that, I don't know if Mr. Hunter would have gotten me to Rich.

December rolled around pretty quickly that fall. Decembers could be hard for me, harder than the other months because of my birthday and Christmas. On the outside, days like that mattered. But in here, you wanted to do your best to forget them— make days like those just like any other kind of day. In an effort to cheer up the place, the Jaycee club would paint backgrounds, though, and put them up in the visitation room and a couple of other areas around the prison. They went by the season, so around Christmastime, they'd hang a big sheet of paper with a fireplace drawn on it; if you wanted, you could take a Polaroid picture in front of it for a couple of bucks, to send to your family. Sitting in front of those painted fireplaces, though, only reminded me how far I was from home. I missed it every day.

That Christmas, my mom and my sisters Tudy, Shelia, and Diane said they were coming to see me. They made a huge home-cooked meal of potato salad, collard greens, smoked chicken, turkey dressing, green beans, and sweet potato pie. I was very excited about their visit. But Christmas Day came and went and I waited for the

COs to call me out, but no call ever came. Later on I learned that my family had been ten minutes late—and since they were not there on time, they had been turned back, dishes of food and all. Shelia told me later that my mother was so upset she couldn't eat a bite of it when they got back.

Rich had sent me an update about a week before Christmas. He wrote,

> Right now I feel pulled in two different directions. On one hand, I'd like to move pretty fast. I think that the judge who is going to be in Alamance County for the next six months would be a good judge to hear your case. I also feel we have a good claim that your appellate counsel was ineffective for failing to raise a claim about the judge keeping the Poole evidence out. Both of these things make me want to file a motion for appropriate relief no later than the middle of February.
>
> On the other hand, my experiences have convinced me that this is probably the only chance we will ever have to put up evidence in your case. In other words, even if we lose and appeal your case for the next ten years, we might never be able to present anything we overlook now. So we need to make sure that we take a very hard look at the entire case to see if there is more investigation we can do . . .

As far as I was concerned, time was the one thing I had plenty of. If what Rich said was true, then this was probably the last chance for the truth to come out. He had explained that the "motion for appropriate relief" was something the lawyers did when all the direct state court appeals were exhausted, something like a Hail Mary play. It was the only way to get into court and have a judge consider certain mistakes that had been made throughout my case. I didn't care how long it took. I wrote Rich back to tell him I put my trust in him and Tom and God. I also told him I didn't feel the first appellate defender had represented my case to the fullest, because he hadn't raised any issue about the all-white jury. I wanted to know what Rich thought of that, but in the end, I trusted they would make the right decisions about when to act in my case. Hell, I wasn't going anywhere.

· · ·

February came and went, and they didn't file the motion. Rich explained that they were being very careful with the timing of everything. In the meantime, the Department of Corrections moved me again in 1993, this time to Harnett, a small penitentiary in Lillington, North Carolina. Every time they moved me, I worried about the trouble that was going to find me. Would I die trying to defend myself? Would I kill someone in self-defense? The pointless violence of the hopeless and those whose minds were not right was always around me. I tried so hard to keep my nose clean so nothing would interfere with my case, should God give me the chance to go before a court of law again.

Rich and Tom sent me many letters about how the investigation was progressing. As far as my evidence went, they explained that legally, it might be nothing more than ashes at this point. Since I had gotten convicted and lost my two appeals, the law said everything could go to the incinerator. They were eager to file a motion to preserve evidence, so that if anything was left, no one could "suggest" that it be destroyed. Toward the end of 1993, Rich told me the motion to preserve evidence had been granted and that they had affidavits from the waitresses at Somer's Seafood who worked with me, who said I had never harassed or touched them while I was there. He also wrote, "I'm not sure that there is anything we can do with the all-white jury suggestion. You and I both know that having an all-white jury can be incredibly prejudicial, especially in a case involving a black defendant and white victims. I just don't see a legal claim based on that here."

Before I knew it, 1993 became 1994, and as much as I tried not to pay attention to the time, there was no getting around the fact that a decade had passed. My brother wrote to tell me our father had had a stroke and was now in a rest home. Life went on—guilty or innocent, crazy or sane, healthy or sick—it just went on. The anger and shock I felt at the beginning left me long ago. I don't want to say I accepted my fate, because it sounds like I gave up. I still prayed to God that I would be free again, but the more I thought about it, the more Diane was right: You had to be free in your heart. Guilt, fear, anger—they were all their own kinds of prison. You could be out in the world and still be doing time. Part of my finding that peace within myself was learning that I was strong enough to carry the load the Lord had asked me to. I knew I would not crack, even if I spent the rest of my life here. The other part was thinking about the women who said I had attacked them. At one point, early on, I had a lot of anger toward them. But in time, I realized they had been through something and made a mistake. They weren't saying I did it because they wanted to hurt me.

Then, in 1994, came the news of O. J. Simpson and the murders of his ex-wife and her boyfriend. At Lillington, I took to standing out in the yard, watching the other inmates, with my back against the wall and my headphones plugged into my radio. Like almost everyone else in prison, I was hooked on news about O. J. Simpson. In the chow halls, out in the yard, it was all anyone talked about: it looked like they were really going to bury the Juice.

On the radio, the news talked a lot about the blood that had been found and some kind of scientific test that was more accurate than anything else. Ninety-nine percent accurate. It was a test called DNA. I tried to learn everything I could about it before I brought it up with Rich.

. . .

Rich and Tom came to visit me at Harnett in Lillington. It was the first time I met Tom Lambeth in person. He was younger than Rich, also on the short side, but a bit more round. He had large glasses and curly brown hair and he smiled a lot for a lawyer.

"Ron, the purpose of us meeting today is to discuss the motion for DNA testing. As you know, we reinvestigated the case from the beginning, and you saw the motion—we think we've got some good legal claims here, where we might win the motion and get you a new trial. But if we ask for DNA, well, it's kind of like be careful what you ask for—"

Tom picked it up from there. "Ron, if that DNA testing puts you there, there's not a judge in the world that's gonna grant our motion. It's over. You're going to stay here. You told us you were innocent and we believe you. But you can never really know as a lawyer. Only you know. We're just here to see what issues we can raise for you. It's fish-or-cut-bait time. Do you really want us to pursue DNA testing?"

Without wavering for a second, I looked them back straight in the eye.

"I promise you I didn't do it. My DNA is not going to be in there." I thought of the hairs they plucked from my head and my pubic area; the blood and the saliva from all those years ago. Would it really be those little things that made all the difference?

After they left, I took my portable radio and my headphones and headed out to the track in the yard. I don't know how many times I walked around and around, looking back in my mind on everything that had happened in the last ten years. The trials, the appeals, the way Poole would pop up somewhere like a weed I couldn't get rid of—all of the legal proceedings felt like spinning circles, too: I went so far only to wind up in the same place I had started. If DNA was as good as they said, it was my last hope of getting out of the ring. When the sun started to go down behind the buildings, a vibe came over me that I was going to leave this place very soon. I headed inside.

• • •

"Mr. Cotton, the Classification Committee is recommending you for transfer to Tennessee. We've got some papers for you to fill out," said one of the prison officials sitting at a table in front of me. It was the end of 1994, and I had been called into an office for a meeting.

I had read in *The News-Observer* that the governor of North Carolina had met with officials from several states, including Rhode Island and Tennessee, to see what could be done about prison over-crowding, but it never occurred to me that I might be one of the in-mates moved.

My mother and father, getting on in the years as they were and in failing health, would not be able to make the eleven-hour drive to Tennessee very easily for a two-hour visit. And even if their health were better, it took money to travel that far. Money that my family didn't have.

"I don't want to go, sir." I said.

"The decision of the Raleigh Committee is not negotiable—"

"What if I refuse this?"

"Mr. Cotton, whether or not you sign these papers, you will be handcuffed, shackled, and if need be, lifted up and placed on that plane to Tennessee."

The Department of Corrections didn't care that a move out of state would make it impossible for my family to visit, and that those visits helped me survive. Like a pinball, I'd already been shot back and forth and up and down the state to four different prisons. And now that I finally had some new attorneys making some progress on my case, they were shipping me out so I couldn't receive visits from them, either. As a consolation, they promised we'd have daily phone privileges in Tennessee.

So within a few months, they shackled me, handcuffed me, and put a chain through my belt loop so that my handcuffs were connected to my leg shackles. I shuffled out to a big old Grey Goose bus and we drove out to Raleigh-Durham airport.

Out on the tarmac, a plane waited for us. As I got off the bus, I noticed on the side of the plane it said, "Express One."

I turned to the guy behind me and nodded at it, "I guess that's because it's only one-way, huh?" Maybe God had a strange sense of humor. This wasn't quite what I had in mind when I got the feeling that I would be leaving Harnett.

It was only my second time on a plane. When I had been very young, I'd ridden on one. The roar of the engines and the feeling that nothing held us to the earth anymore had scared me so much I'd urinated on myself. I decided that this was probably not a good story to tell the guy I sat next to.

There were three rows of three, filled with male and female inmates. I had a window seat. We lifted up, and I watched Raleigh and the rest of North Carolina grow small below us. The fields and ponds I'd played in, the woods I'd chased my brothers and sisters through, the dirt roads we had flown down in my father's car, waiting for the bumps that would send us shooting off the seat, all of it faded below the clouds until I couldn't see anything. Eleven years and seven hundred miles from home, I wondered if the next time I touched North Carolina soil, my body would be in a box.

We landed on a Tennessee air force base about an hour or so later. They loaded up all the men on a couple of buses, making us get on starting from the back to the front, filling the seats. After we filed on, a bald-headed guy with a big old Buddha belly stepped on. He stood up front and stared at us. I could read the letters "WTDC" on his shirt.

"Y'all from North Carolina? Y'all think you're bad? That's because you ain't been to Tennessee yet."

When we pulled in to West Tennessee Detention Center, Buddha Belly stood up again.

"Welcome to your new home, ladies. There're some COs that can't wait to get to know ya. We're going to get real cozy real fast."

They strip-searched us, and then sent us off to our assigned bunks. There were about eighty people to a dorm, two bunks high. I didn't even bother to fill out a visitation list, because I knew I would not have any visitors.

. . .

I took a job in the prison laundry and did everything I could to stay under the radar and focus on what Rich and Tom were trying to do in my case. Rich sent me a copy of the motion for appropriate relief they had mailed to the clerk in Alamance County. Rich explained it was the State of North Carolina's way of giving me one more shot at a trial because enough evidence had come up postconviction that made it seem as if I didn't have a fair trial.

It was a huge document, with affidavits signed by Phil and Dan and the waitresses I had worked with at Somer's Seafood, who said I never did anything improper, and a whole chart studying the patterns in Bobby Poole's crimes and how they were similar to the rapes of the two women I had been convicted for. Now, I wasn't a lawyer or a judge, but I was mighty impressed.

In August, Rich informed me that he and Tom had gone down to the Burlington Police Department to see what evidence was still there. They met with one of the detectives who had interrogated me, Mike Gauldin, and the evidence custodian. Detective Gauldin had turned over the box of evidence and said, "You know it's just going to prove what we already know. Cotton did it."

Tom said he'd just smiled politely and replied, "We'll see about that."

. . .

A few months later, Rich wrote to tell me that the order for DNA testing was approved. They had gone with the ADA into the judge's chambers and said they weren't trying to pull any tricks. They just wanted to know the truth, once and for all. Rich told me the Assistant DA Rob Johnson seemed like a good guy but he told him if the DNA tests came back and put me at the crime scenes, he expected the motion to go away. It was just past Christmas, and his letter was a gift that lifted my spirits. There was a new year just around the corner.

I went back to the waiting game. Waiting for news, thinking about what might or might not be, I started having nightmares. I had the same one, over and over. I was in the swimming hole in Glen Raven. Out in the water, I felt myself getting sucked down again. There were people standing on the bank, and I called out for them to help me but I had no voice, nothing came out. I was getting so tired trying to swim out of the hole. Then I noticed the water felt sticky, and all of the sudden I realized it was blood. I'd wake up with my heart pounding like rain on a tin roof.

I don't know what I was more afraid of: the fact that this was my last shot at freedom and it could all backfire like it had before, or that it might work, and I would finally walk out into the world again. The struggle for justice all these years had made me grow up and take responsibility for myself; it had given my life a focus. Whichever way the decision went, when the battle was done I wasn't sure what I'd do with myself.

Flipping to the dog-eared pages of my Bible, I read from the Book of Psalms to ease my mind.

> *In thee, O LORD, do I put my trust: let me never be put to confusion.*

Deliver me in thy righteousness, and cause me to escape:
*   incline thine ear unto me, and save me.*
Deliver me, O my God, out of the hand of the wicked, out
*   of the hand of the unrighteous and cruel man.*

· · ·

Early in 1995, Rich wrote to let me know that the State Bureau of Investigation's lab did not have the ability to perform the DNA test, but that there was a private lab that could do it, and the evidence was already in their hands. My father, being in the nursing home, couldn't help out financially but somehow the test was going to get done anyway.

Then a few months later, Rich and I got to talk on the phone. He told me that he and Tom had been to a meeting at the lab in Raleigh to view the results of the DNA test on the Reynolds case.

"It's not a match, Ron. Your markers weren't in there." I thought this was good news, but something in his voice told me it wasn't all good, so I waited for him to go on. "Unfortunately the lab folks haven't been able to identify any DNA at all from the Thompson case samples aside from hers and her boyfriend's."

"Mr. Rosen, what does that mean?"

"Well, Ron, it doesn't clear you. They didn't find DNA that was yours, but they also didn't find any mystery DNA. There's just no evidence either way, so we're still left with litigating that case. The lab will file a report and, hopefully, we'll get a date set for the hearing. We're going to ask the court to consider the DNA evidence from the Reynolds case hearing as newly discovered evidence in the Thompson case. Basically, as the Supreme Court held in your first appeal, it is extremely likely that the same person committed both crimes, so evidence that proves you didn't commit the Reynolds attack is powerful new evidence that you did not commit the Thompson attack."

I thought of the two trials, and Jennifer Thompson telling the jury she was sure it was me. I worried that her words were stronger than any kind of scientific test.

"It's frustrating, I know, but we'll see what we can do. You take care of yourself, Ron. I'll be in touch as things develop."

I didn't know how much more my nerves could take. I resolved to put the case out of my mind. There was nothing more I could do now.

May 16, 1995

Dear Mr. Rosen:

Sir, we know that this matter at hand is very serious and it's been a long time since this case has been worked on. I really appreciate the effort you have put into this case, not to mention Tom, etc.

I'm glad things are still looking good and hopefully all goes well and this case will be before some judge. Mr. Rosen, I have made up in my mind not to worry about anything that's taken place in this case right now. I will soon be incarcerated eleven years coming August and if I should be released today from prison, I'd be one lost young man. . . .

PART 3

Jennifer
and Ronald

CHAPTER 11

Jennifer

THE SPRING DAY the phone rang, I had already cleaned most of the house, in as much as you can keep a house clean when you have three almost-five-year-olds who mark their paths by shedding toys from room to room. I was down in the playroom, surrounded by Playmobil toys and Matchbox cars, when the trill of the phone shot through from the guest bedroom.

I stepped into the room. My husband and I referred to it as the "costume department" because I had filled the closet in there with outfits from thrift stores that the kids could dress up in, create plays around: the Cruella De Vil dress, the G.I. Joe shirt, the Russian czar coat. "Hello?"

"Jennifer? It's Mike Gauldin."

"Mike! How are you? How's Karen?" I said. It had probably

been at least a year since we had spoken, but I would have recognized his voice instantly even if he hadn't told me who was calling.

"Good, good. We're good. How about you?"

"Vinny's busy finishing up his master's degree, the kids are getting ready to 'graduate,' and I'm probably washing my hundredth pound of laundry this week."

" 'Graduate?' "

"From preschool. They start kindergarten in the fall," I explained.

"Kindergarten! Where does the time go?" He laughed, and paused a minute. "Jennifer, I've got something to talk to you about. I'd like to come by."

"Well, sure, you know I'd love to see you."

"How's tomorrow, then?"

Were it not for the fact that I was talking to Mike, whose very voice calmed me, and the three small children I had in the next room, I might have completely panicked. Tomorrow? Something was up. Mike was now captain at the Burlington Police Department, and he certainly wasn't coming to see how the kids were doing.

"Wow. OK. Is everything all right?"

"Everything's fine. We just need to talk in person. I'm bringing the assistant district attorney with me. How's eleven?"

"Eleven is fine. See you then."

I hung up the phone and stared at it sitting dumbly in its cradle. I looked out the window into the backyard of the house I shared in Winston-Salem with my husband Vinny, our triplets, and our dog, Bingo. My son Blake's protesting voice drifted in from the playroom, followed by peals of his sisters' laughter. Poor Blake never had a choice—he had to do what Brittany and Morgan wanted to do or else they excluded him. My stomach cramped. *Had Ronald Cotton escaped? Was he coming up for parole? Were we all in danger?*

· · ·

When the first trial ended in 1985 and they took Ronald Cotton away for life, everyone expected me to "move on." Instead, I fell apart.

Paul and I had been fighting constantly, and we both knew we were not going to make it. It would have been in extremely poor taste for him, being such a small town and all, to not be there with me through the trial. But just a month later, we mutually agreed to end things. Paul had been so afraid to look at me a certain way or touch me a certain way, or say something a certain way, and I guess in the end I felt like he couldn't get over it. He wanted to graduate from business school, return to Burlington, and be looked up to in the community I loathed. And I'm sure he probably thought, but would never admit, *what kind of wife and mother would I, the traumatized rape victim, be?*

I tried to focus on finishing my final semester of school so I could get the heck out of Burlington as soon as I graduated. As part of my requirements for graduating, I took an internship at a state-of-the-art health club in Greensboro. The tennis instructor there was a guy named Vic, who was tall with curly blond hair and dimples, clean-cut, athletic, and polite. It didn't take long for me to develop a crush on him. I wasn't looking for anything serious, but maybe part of the road back for me was having a relationship with a nice guy. If I could do that, I thought, maybe it meant I wasn't so damaged.

One night, I was in my apartment in Burlington and someone came knocking on my door. I asked who was there, and he said, "It's me, Vic." My heart sped up with excitement; I was so flattered. I opened the door and he came stumbling in. We sat downstairs and talked and it became clear that he was really inebriated. I told him I needed him to leave. He begged me to let him stay the night. "Please, I'm so drunk. I can't drive," he slurred at me. I finally agreed he could stay on my couch.

I brought him a blanket and some water, and then I went upstairs to bed. I was in there maybe twenty minutes or so when, all of a sudden, Vic opened my door and climbed into bed with me.

I had to fight him off and it was truly a physical fight. I screamed and kicked and pushed, until he got up off me, calling me "tease" and "slut," weaving his way down the stairs to the door. "Get the fuck out, you son of a bitch!" I yelled. "Get out!" I bolted the door behind him and threw my fist at the door, then slid down the front of it, hugging my knees to my chest and weeping.

I called a girlfriend from the health club, one who was always up for partying. She drove over and we drank beer, and I cried some more and went on about how much I hated men. At some point, the decision was made to go get some coke. So we got in my car and drove to Chapel Hill around 2:00 A.M., to a basement student apartment, a friend of her friend's. A young man opened the door. There were lots of people inside his apartment. I handed over fifty dollars and he handed me a small plastic bag. He didn't let go of it, though. He narrowed his eyes at me. "Don't tell anybody where you got this," he said. I nodded, and he released the bag.

Back at my apartment, my friend decided we should invite more people over to party. I inhaled my lines and told myself I was getting everything under control. I felt the numbness on my teeth and the back of my throat spread. I hated myself, and I hated my life, but for a short time, the coke made me not care. I simply shrugged, and until seven or eight the next morning, various people I did not know dropped by my apartment to drink beer and do coke, disappearing for a while upstairs. When the sunlight began streaming in, my friend left with a guy and my apartment was empty. I left the beer cans and full ashtrays on the table and went up to my bed. At least the night was over.

I was supposed to work at 2:00 P.M., but I couldn't get out of bed. I lay there for hours crying, disgusted with myself. I stared at the phone, knowing I should pick it up and mumble an excuse about being sick, but I didn't care. The entire day I stayed in bed, crying. I decided that day even though I was not going to marry Paul and I was not graduating with a 4.0, I had to re-create myself, somehow. Because if I went on like this, I would kill myself. And if I died, it would mean that the moment when Ronald Cotton sprung up from the darkness and into my life threatening to kill me, had defined me. It would mean he had won, that he really did kill me that night. And I hated him too much to let him win.

A few weeks later, a girl I knew from Elon convinced me to go down to Florida with her for spring break. "It'll be good for you," she said. Looking back now, I can't believe I had just come out of a rape trial and agreed to go to Fort Lauderdale. I went down there with the absolute worst intestinal flu in my life and never left my room for the first three days. Instead, I stared out through the balcony doors at the drab squatness of the cheap hotels surrounding us, listening to the noise that rose up from the streets: gunning motorcycles, hooting frat boys, and squealing women that muted even the crashing surf shimmering on the horizon.

When I ventured out at last, I wore gray jeans, a sweater, and white sneakers, hoping I would not attract any kind of sexual attention. In fact, among all the miniskirts and girls in halter tops, I hoped I was invisible. While my friend and her boyfriend got airbrushed shirts with their names on them, I stepped inside a bar so I wouldn't be standing out in the street with roaming packs of drunken men and women.

But I was only there for a few minutes when a dark-haired guy wearing sunglasses came up to me and said, "Hey, can I get you a drink?" I thought he was cute. He reminded me of Don Johnson, so I said, "Sure." Instead of returning to the bar, he simply handed me his. A comedian, I thought. I held his half-full drink and looked at him like, thanks. Then he said, "You want a cigarette?" And I said, "Sure," to play along, so he took the one he was smoking and handed it to me. Then he asked me if I wanted to dance. I laughed and said, "Are you going to stand there and dance for me now?"

He grinned at me, took the drink and the cigarette and put them down, and grabbed me by the hand. "No, let's really dance," he said.

As we danced, we talked about where we were from. He was a graphic designer from Long Island, and he knew a girl I had gone to high school with. He was extremely polite. When the song ended, I told him I needed to get back to my friends, and he asked me if he could take me to dinner the next night. Guys on spring break didn't do that, so I was intrigued.

I told him we could go to dinner but if he touched me, I'd kill him. He put his hands up in the air in surrender and said, "You got it."

We met up the following evening in the hotel restaurant. He ordered a strawberry daiquiri and steak and green beans, although I don't know why since he proceeded to try and eat the chicken off my plate. I had never met anybody like him. He wore sunglasses and dangled a cigarette from his lips when he wasn't chewing Clorets gum. He wore a blazer with a T-shirt and he made me laugh. We kissed at the end of the night, and it was a kiss that made me feel innocent and hopeful again. It wasn't a kiss that demanded more, that pushed and prodded. I told him I was leaving the next day, and he asked me if he could take my friend and me to lunch before we left.

The next day, he was so sunburned from lying out that he looked like a lobster, albeit a lobster with moussed hair and a calculated few days of stubble. He was still cute, even though he looked absolutely ridiculous. We had open-faced turkey sandwiches for lunch and played shuffleboard, and I gave him my address and phone number and didn't think too much about it. Figured I'd fly home and that would be it. It would just be a story: I'd met a guy named Vinny from New York.

But I don't think I was home for six hours when the phone started ringing and it was Vinny. We probably talked about every three hours for the first few weeks. And he wrote to me every day. The next month, he flew down to see me. He was absolutely crazy about me. He didn't jump on me and innately seemed to sense that I needed to be treated delicately.

The following month, I decided to fly up to Long Island to visit him. I knew I had to tell him what had happened to me, because if he couldn't deal with it, I didn't want to invest anything more into Vinny from New York. We went on a walk from his house toward the canals in Brightwater, a flat, eight-mile walk. At times, we could see clear to the ocean. I told him that I had been raped at my college, and my case had gone to trial. I braced myself for hostility and judgment, but there was none. "What happened to the guy?" he asked.

"He got life in prison," I said.

"Good. That's what he deserves," he said. We had stopped right in front of a Friendly's, and as he held me tight, I stared at the window where you could walk up and order an ice-cream cone. Was Vinny really strong enough to hold on to me? Or would he run away, the way Paul had? The sacred lie in my "moving on" was that I had simply learned to live with the continued presence of Ronald Cotton, pushing him to the edges of my life when I could.

By June when I graduated, with Vincent telling me how in love with me he was, we made a plan that I would move up to Long Island to be with him. I was desperate to get as far away from Burlington as I could. I excitedly packed up my apartment, and in those final days, Paul dropped by to say good-bye.

"I just want you to know," he said, "that I'm so sorry for the way things turned out. I still really care about you, Jennifer. I always will."

"Me, too," I said, and we hugged each other.

"I wish things had been different."

"Me, too," I said.

"I never even told you but I had already put our names into the lottery for married student housing," he said.

We both felt the sting in that, at how close we had once been to making those kinds of decisions, and how life had jumped the tracks because of a violent assault, not something we had chosen. In the end, we were both cheated. It was incredibly painful. I drove off with Burlington in my rearview mirror, eager to start a new life with Vinny.

But as safe as I felt with Vinny, I hated Long Island. I missed the South terribly and told Vinny I was returning to North Carolina, with or without him. He told me I was his future, and he would go wherever I needed to be. When the ground thawed, we were gone. By spring of 1986, we moved into a condo in Winston-Salem and I got a job in a bank.

Vinny was creative and intelligent, and if darkness ever seized me, he could always crack me up and shake me out of it, by running into a wall or suddenly falling on the floor. We did everything together: cleaned the house, hunted for antiques, took long walks. If I wanted him, he never left my side.

One afternoon, as we were folding the laundry, Vinny said to me, "I've been wondering about something . . ."

"What?" I said.

"I've been wondering, Jennifer, would you marry me?"

I laughed at him, because I wasn't sure if this was another of his jokes.

"Are you serious?"

"I am most serious. Go look in the closet in your shoe," he said.

I gave him a skeptical look and went to my closet, where I found a diamond ring inside one of my shoes.

He encircled me from behind. "So how about it?"

I turned to face him, tears in my eyes. "Yes, Vinny from New York, I will marry you."

A few months into our engagement, Mike Gauldin called me to say there would be another trial. I was shocked. I had no idea Ronald Cotton could have his conviction overturned. I was scared to death he'd go free. But Mike told me this time, they would be trying my case together with the case of the second woman who had been assaulted that night. While I told Mike of course I would be there to testify, I resented it. I talked little of my rape to anyone in my new life; there was no need for people to know. And now here it came again. I had to explain to my boss at the bank that I would need to be out for a while, that last time the trial had lasted two weeks.

The DA's office put me up in a little creepy place that Vinny and I called the Bates Motel. I was terrified there, terrified that Ronald Cotton's family knew where I was and would come after me, despite the police stationed in the parking lot and Vinny at my side. In that awful avocado and gold room with the shag rug, in the town I had avoided like the plague, Vinny managed my extremes of "don't touch me but don't leave me" the best he could.

The new prosecutor, Luke Turner, was very different from Jim Roberson. He was aloof, and didn't appear interested in my emotional state, only how I could serve his case. I remember thinking the second woman was going to blow it and Ronald Cotton was going to walk. Mary Reynolds cried a lot and became very distraught to the point where she didn't make any sense.

It was very difficult to hear what Mary had been through, and I was furious during the voir dire, that Ronald Cotton's defense attorneys would try to point the finger at someone else, using a jailhouse snitch to do it, no less. There was never a doubt in my mind, that Ronald Cotton was the man who assaulted me. It felt like they were just dragging things out.

I watched bailiffs take Ronald Cotton away for a second time, his original sentence augmented by another term of life. *Good riddance, bastard,* I thought. *May you burn in hell.* Luke Turner thanked me for a job well done with a shake of the hand, and Mike hugged me and told me I deserved all the happiness in the world.

About a year later, Vinny and I got married. Then in 1989, I discovered I was pregnant. I went in to the doctor, who put me at twelve weeks, yet I had already gained twenty-one pounds. "What the heck are you eating?" the doctor joked. The holiday season was coming, and he warned me to lay off the cookies and pie. But by Christmas, I needed to wear a full maternity dress. Vinny knew I wasn't eating that much, and at eighteen weeks he accompanied me back to the doctor's for a sonogram. While we waited for the doctor in the examining room, we joked that I would be the woman on the cover of *Newsweek* giving birth to a twenty-five-pound baby—it was either that or a fully grown four-year-old. I was that big.

The nurse came in and apologized that the doctor was running late. I had to pee incredibly badly, because they made me drink a ton of water before the sonogram. Finally the doctor came in and said the woman before me was having twins; that was the reason for his delay. They smeared the cold jelly on my enormous globe of a stomach and we all stared at the screen. But the screen simply remained black, as the nurse moved the instrument around, trying to find something. "I can't find anything," she said. The doctor told me to void half my bladder, and I returned only to have the same thing happen: a black screen telling us nothing. Finally, the doctor instructed me to empty my bladder completely. This time, the doctor himself performed the sonogram. We all peered intently at the screen, until finally, some gray blobs appeared.

"Oh, my goodness! Twins!" he suddenly said. The nurse and Vinny and I all stared at the monitor. "Here's baby A's head, and heart, and feet, and there, you see that, that's baby B's head, heart, and little feet."

I looked to Vinny to see if I could read his emotions, but Vinny was still staring at the monitor.

"So if those are baby A's feet, and those are baby B's," he said, "whose foot is that?" He pointed to the upper corner of the screen.

The nurse looked at him skeptically. "What are you talking about?"

And this time the doc scanned up. "Oh my God," the nurse said. "There's another baby!"

At this point, I did not want them to do any more scanning. I mean, how many could be in there? We were elated and in shock at the same time. I got dressed and we sat in the doctor's office. Bed rest, doctor's orders. So I returned home to wait and wait as I grew bigger and bigger.

At thirty-two weeks, I went to the hospital. There are pictures of me, clutching a sixty-four-ounce bottle of Maalox, wearing a brightly colored muumuu and looking as if there was no part of me that hadn't expanded or stretched. The nurses would come in to roll me to one side to wash me, and then roll me to the other. For two weeks, I did not move from the bed but seemed to grow by the minute, and finally, at thirty-four weeks, they performed a C-section. I had three beautiful babies, each so different and each so perfect. Morgan was tow headed, blue eyed, and coltish; Brittany, brunette, with deep brown eyes like mine that seemed intense and introspective from the day she was born; and my son Blake had the dark good looks and charm of his father.

With our triple dose of happiness, we moved into a brick ranch house on Archer Road in Winston-Salem. There was nothing grand about it, but I had everything I wanted: a fenced-in yard, a bedroom across the hall from my babies, and a little deck off the kitchen where we laid down AstroTurf and put up netting so Morgan, Brittany, and Blake could play outside and not get splinters. It was a happy house, a house where I kissed away scraped knees and bee stings, a house where they wrote their first words in chalk on the sidewalk out front.

Only at night, when the kids were sleeping soundly in their beds and Vinny slumbered at my side, would I still shake with fear, hearing footsteps in the house, seeing shapes in the dark. And always his face. The hateful face of Ronald Cotton floating above mine. I prayed hard for the kids, that I could keep them safe. As long as he was locked away for life, he couldn't hurt us, I reminded myself. Over the years, my nighttime fear subsided somewhat. But I still prayed each and every day for Ronald Cotton's violent death. Only then did I think that awful face might retreat back into the shadowy evil he had emerged from and I would finally be free.

So what the hell could Mike be coming to tell me?

. . .

Vinny stayed home the next day so he could be there when Mike Gauldin and Rob Johnson arrived. The kids were at preschool, right around the corner, at the same place where I had gone to kindergarten.

I opened the door and hugged Mike. Mike shook hands with Vinny, and then he introduced us to Rob Johnson. Rob was shorter than Mike, dressed beautifully in a blue suit. He had a round face, with brown hair thinning on the top and graying at the temples, and he had large, wire-framed glasses. He reminded me of Tommy Lee Jones.

Mike looked like he had barely aged. He still had a thick head of wavy brown hair. About the only thing that showed the passage of eleven years were the lines that fanned out from the corners of his eyes. He had on a pair of slacks and a brown tweed jacket, with a blue button-down.

I suggested we sit out on the back porch. It was a warm day for March, and I brought out some iced tea and glasses on a tray. It's funny the pleasantries you try to maintain in an effort to keep the anxiety, which wants to run around the room breaking things, under control. We sipped our iced tea and talked about the sunshine, the weather, and current events. Vinny and I looked at the two men, waiting.

"Look, Jennifer, I hate bringing this up, but Ronald Cotton has some new attorneys, and they filed a motion and we feel that we need to cooperate with it."

My anger and disgust turned the sweet tea bitter. When would this ever go away?

"Well, what does that have to do with me?" I said. "I don't want to go back to court. I can't go again. I'm finally getting to a point where I can put this past me, and I've got small kids now."

"They want to have some testing done," Mike said, looking to Rob Johnson for help.

"Mrs. Cannino, have you ever heard of DNA?" Rob said.

"Like the O. J. Simpson stuff?"

"That's exactly right. There's a new test that can analyze biological evidence in the rape kit, and it's very accurate," Rob said.

"Ronald Cotton has asked for a DNA test to be done on the rape kit," Mike informed me. "The problem is your blood sample has disintegrated since 1984. We need a new sample of blood from you, so we can figure out what DNA belongs to you and what DNA belongs to the man who attacked you."

"You know, every time I think I'm really moving on, something pulls me back. The other night, Vinny and I were watching basketball and one of the players—Scottie Pippen—his face. I made Vinny turn it off because he looked so much like Ronald Cotton to me, and no matter how far I think I get, I still wake up from nightmares with that face in my mind."

Mike is the kind of guy who loved being a cop because he loved helping people, and I could tell that this day was one of the few in his life when he probably hated his job. "We hope this test will put it to rest forever," he said.

"But why? Why do I have to do this? Why do I have to go through this again?" I asked. "I'm supposed to be the victim."

"Mrs. Cannino, it's important for you to know you don't *have* to consent to a blood sample," Rob said. "At least not yet. But his attorneys could get a court order down the line."

"Look, we all know it's not going to change anything. It's just a last attempt. We got the right guy," Mike said. "Ronald Cotton is going to stay put in prison. But they could drag this thing out . . ."

I couldn't believe how unfair it all was, that a twice-convicted rapist who was supposed to be sent away to die in prison could keep messing with my life. Weren't the two trials enough? There was a part of me that wanted to say, "Screw it, his lawyers are going to have to come with a search warrant before they get a drop of my blood." And this, I thought, looking out at our neatly mowed lawn and the tricycle parked by the garden, this is *mine*, and Ronald Cotton has no right to encroach on any of it. Still, the thought that this would go on any longer—that it would keep coming back into my life—was enough to make me agree. If this would finally make it go away, then I'd comply.

I looked up at them. "OK. I'll do it, but I want to do it right away. Can you take it today?"

Rob and Mike looked at each other with a mixture of surprise and relief. Relief, because I think they wanted this to go away as quickly as possible, too, but thought I might need some time to stew over it.

Mike said he would make a few calls.

In the end, law enforcement officials from Forsyth County gave Mike a rape kit, and they drove me to my doctor's office in downtown Winston-Salem. Vinny stayed home so he could pick up the kids from preschool and feed them lunch. Mike drove and Rob insisted I sit in front, so he got in the backseat. Passing Forsyth Hospital, I pointed at it and told them it was where I had had the kids.

I watched the vial fill up with my blood; it only took a minute and then the nurse capped it and placed it in a bag and gave it to Mike. We exited the medical building and Mike said, "We should get you some food." He looked around, and I guess we all saw the Pie Works pizza place across the street at the same time. "Pizza?" he said.

With my blood in a bag between them, Rob and Mike sat on one side of a booth and I sat on the other, and we tore into a large cheese pizza with half and half toppings: half black bean for me, and half meat for the guys.

Mike and Rob dropped me off at home a half hour later. When I walked into the house, I heard "Mommeeee!" and suddenly had three babies throw themselves at me. I bent down to scoop them up in my arms, hugging them tight and breathing in the wonderful clean downiness of their hair.

It was done.

CHAPTER 12

Ronald

June 1995

"COTTON, C'MERE A MINUTE. The warden wants to see you," said a CO, calling me to the door. He was a friendly black guy, about five foot seven, with a thick mustache and curly hair.

I was in my dorm for the night, having finished work and had my shower. I was relaxing with some of the other guys, watching TV. A couple of them raised their eyebrows at me. The only time you go to the warden is for discipline—I couldn't think of any rules or regulations I had broken, or anything I had witnessed. I got up and locked my locker before heading over to the CO, worried that there had been a death in the family. It was the only other possibility.

The warden's office had a couple of filing cabinets, and a big brown wooden desk. The warden sat behind it with the look of a man who had something on his mind. He was white, on the skinny side, with brownish blond hair and a mustache. He was wearing a blue-striped shirt. He leaned back in his leather chair.

"Have a seat," he said, gesturing at the metal chair in front of his desk.

He nodded at the corrections officer who brought me in; the officer stepped outside and waited in the hallway.

"Mr. Cotton, I've got good news and bad news. Which do you want to hear first?"

I took a deep breath. "The bad news." I prepared myself, looking around at the framed certificates on the wall and the print of flowers that no doubt was supposed to cheer up the place. One of my sisters had written me earlier to tell me that she had ended up in the hospital after she had some trouble with her boyfriend. I could not help but wonder if the warden was about to tell me my sister had been killed.

"Bad news is you're going back to court," he said.

While I was relieved that the warden did not tell me anyone had died, I wasn't sure what to think about going back to court. Given my history, going back to court might not be a good thing. Who knows? Maybe there were new charges against me, more women that had said I raped them.

I looked at him, waiting for the second part.

"The good news is the guy that committed the crime you're doing time for confessed. You're going home tomorrow."

I couldn't speak. Was he bullshitting me? How could I be here all these years and then, just like that, I'm going home tomorrow? It made me suspicious. I doubted Poole had suddenly gotten a conscience. I wished I could talk to my attorneys.

The warden leaned forward in his seat, placing his arms on the desk. "And because you're going home, what I want you to do for me is tell me what officers are running the drugs in here. I know you know. Just tell me their names."

I looked back at him, thinking how friendly he was trying to be, like we were one and the same, guys who would do each other favors.

I knew a lot of officers that did things for certain inmates they trusted, things they didn't have to, things they could have lost their jobs for. One of the older COs from Greensboro used to pass me a can of Budweiser every now and then. "Got a son in prison," he used to say.

"I'm not going to be your snitch," I said. "If you want to find out, that's your job."

The warden's friendliness quickly disappeared. Obviously, he was a man used to getting what he wanted. He was not happy at all.

"Take him back to his dorm," he yelled to the CO outside. As the CO walked me back, I tried to ask him if he knew anything more. "Can't say as I know you're going home, but I do know for sure you're going back to court," he said. That really hit me. The motion Rich had filed—they must have got me a new trial. Even if I was going back for yet another trial, at least I'd be housed in Graham, near my family.

When I returned to the dorm, I looked at all the guys sitting around, on their bunks, at the table, waiting for time to pass. I think the grin on my face stretched from Tennessee to North Carolina. I spotted a buddy.

"Man, they said I'm going home tomorrow," I told him. "For real."

"You serious? I knew you were telling the truth, I always knew you were innocent. I'm real glad for you, man."

A couple more COs came over and told me to prepare my belongings because the North Carolina police would be coming to transport me in the morning. I went over to my locker and put everything in it on my bunk. I stared at all I had accumulated: by now I had three radios, boxes of Dentyne gum, and enough soap to last me maybe ten years, canteen supplies. I also had a list of people who owed me money for canteen items.

I took the list and one of my radios and found Blair, one of the guys who helped me out.

"Look, man, I'm going back to North Carolina. So take this. If you collect the money, it's yours, but don't get into any trouble collecting. If they can't pay, let it slide. And here," I said, handing him the radio I used to rent out for a dollar a night, "this is for you."

I took more of my stuff from my bunk, and started handing it out to the guys in my dorm like it was Christmas and I was Santa. Jeremy, a long-haired white dude who was always in trouble for fighting, looked at me like I was nuts when I handed him another radio. A while back, he had stuck me in the arm with a pencil, although no lead had stuck. I knew he had nothing, no family. A young guy named Porter got the other radio. Some of the inmates gave me pictures of themselves, signed "Good luck," along with their names. I think they were afraid they'd be forgotten.

In the end, all I decided to take for myself was a toothbrush and six months' worth of soap. I figured, no matter what, I still needed to keep my teeth clean and my body fresh. I took another shower and lay on my bunk. I didn't sleep a wink but lay awake all night, wondering what was really going to happen when I went back to North Carolina.

• • •

In the morning, COs got me and brought me to a holding cell, and then two officers from the Asheville prison unit in North Carolina came to pick me up. They went through my stuff to make sure I wasn't taking any contraband, and then they handcuffed me and put me in the back of a squad car. I wore a white T-shirt with a blue collar and a white pair of pants, the outfit the WTDC gave to its inmates who worked in the kitchen. It was clean, at least. My hair had grown pretty long so I had a decent Afro; there was just no time to cut it.

They put my bag of soap, pictures, and letters in the trunk. They were two young guys, probably both in their early thirties. In fact, I thought we could be neck-to-neck in age.

They wore sunglasses and full uniforms down to their shiny boots. One of them, the one with dark brown hair, drove the car. He had a strap around the back of his head to hold the sunglasses on. I thought I'd probably stare at that strap for many hours. We had a long drive. The other guy in the passenger seat had lighter brown hair. He broke the silence and turned.

"We heard about your case," he said.

The driver looked at me in his rearview. "Is it true you spent eleven years locked up for something you didn't do?"

"Yes, sir," I said.

"That's messed up," he said, shaking his head.

A couple of hours into the trip, the officers talked about being hungry, and where they should stop to eat. They exited off the freeway where there was a sign for gas and food.

"Let's go to McDonald's," the one in the passenger seat said.

The driver pulled into the parking lot and parked the car. He turned to look at me over his shoulder. "You hungry?" he asked.

I told him I was. I asked for a Quarter Pounder with Cheese and fries, and the officer with the lighter hair went in to order while the dark-haired one and I sat down at a table outside. I placed my hands on the table.

"Sorry about those," said the dark-haired officer, looking down at the handcuffs on my wrists. "Just following the protocol for transporting you."

I looked around and noticed a couple a few tables away, staring at me. I'm sure they were wondering what the hell was going on, with a man in handcuffs sitting at McDonald's. It was my first realization that people on the outside were going to have a lot of trouble understanding what had happened to me, since I didn't have a sign that read "innocent" on my forehead. And of course, I didn't look very innocent sitting there with handcuffs and an armed police officer.

The other officer came over and set a tray down in front of me. I will never forget that first whiff of McDonald's fries after eleven years. It was exactly as I remembered it, and yet it had never tasted so good before. It didn't take very long for me to get down my lunch.

The officers laughed at me and asked if I wanted some more. I told them I didn't. I was so nervous and excited and jittery, I knew

I had to pace myself or else I'd be sick. They also told me more about what they knew.

"We're really sorry for what happened to you; that guy shouldn't have waited so long," the light-haired one said, referring to Poole. "Even after the DNA linked him, it still took him five hours to confess, that's what I heard."

"What a sorry S.O.B.," said the other one.

I was not surprised. Poole was not going to step up willingly to take responsibility for the crimes. That was clear long ago. God was finally taking care of things, just like my father had said.

"So listen, you're going home but tonight you've got to stay in the Asheville prison because of the court schedule. Tomorrow we will take you to Alamance County and release you into their custody."

"I know it seems kind of odd, but it's just one more night, right?" said the light-haired one.

I didn't have a choice, and they were right: what was one more night after I had spent so many behind bars?

But that night in the Asheville prison, time had suddenly slowed down. There was a leaky sink in the cell and each drop would have to grow to a certain size before it was heavy enough to spill off into the sink. I could feel every minute like that, time collecting around itself until it was heavy enough to pass. I wanted to sleep, but I was too excited. I hadn't even bothered to make up my bunk. I just got on the bare mattress and pulled the blanket over me, fully dressed with my shoes on. My feet hung over the edge of the bed, like I was a fireman waiting on a bell.

The same two officers came to get me when the sun came out. It climbed in the sky as we drove along the highway, promising a beautiful day. My mind still wondered if I was really going to be freed or if it was just a time cut—a reduction on my sentence—and I'd be imprisoned again back in North Carolina.

• • •

The car rolled into downtown Graham, where the big courthouse with the statue in front of it rose up in front of us.

"This the courthouse?" the light-haired cop said.

"That's where I was sentenced, but the district court is down the road." I knew from the jailer in Asheville that I would not be going to the Superior Court, but the new district court.

I couldn't shake the fear that somehow this was a trick, that maybe I was being indicted on more charges. I had made this journey twice before. But this time, we did not stop at the big marble courthouse in the middle of the traffic circle, which looked like it was watching you and judging you no matter which way around it you went. The police car continued down Elm Street, to a brick building that housed a new court. And that's when I saw the news trucks. It was Friday, June 30, 1995. I learned later that Fridays at district court are called "zoo days" because it's the day when non-police cases are tried. It's just people—mothers and fathers making private charges against each other. But it became my Good Friday.

The officers took me in with my bag and processed me. "Ronald Cotton is no longer in custody of the Department of Corrections. He is now in the custody of the Alamance County Sheriff's Office." A female bailiff received me into custody, and put her handcuffs on me.

The dark-haired officer spoke up. "That really necessary?"

"I'm not taking those cuffs off," she said. "You want 'em off, the judge got to say so."

The dark-haired cop looked at another bailiff, and he left to go find the judge.

The judge came into the recess room. It was the same man who had presided over my probable cause hearing in August 1984, the same man who had increased the bond on all of my charges individually. His hair was now almost purely white but still thick. He wore glasses and had a sharp, pointy nose like a beak.

He didn't say a word to me but told the female bailiff, "I give you a direct order to take the handcuffs off him." He waited until she had put them in the leather pouch on her belt, then swept out of the room.

"Good luck," said the Asheville officers and left. Next, a male bailiff with hair slicked back like Dracula brought me in a bag of clothes. "This is from your family; you can go into the restroom and change."

"My family's here?" I said.

He nodded.

Inside the bathroom, I put on a purple shirt and black jeans; later I would learn my sister Tudy had gone shopping for them. The purple shirt hangs in my closet to this day.

I sat in my new clothes waiting, as maybe fifteen or twenty minutes went by. Then the bailiff came back to get me. "You ready?" he said. I nodded.

He brought me into the courtroom. It was much smaller than the one I had been tried and convicted in. And I realized immediately the news cameras were here for me. Tom and Rich stood at the defense table, and just behind them, my family. I did not see the women who had said I attacked them, only the faces of my mother, Diane, Tudy, Shelia, and some of my nephews. They beamed at me with happiness.

A district attorney I had never seen before was opposite from us.

The hearing was very short. Tom and Rich presented their motion for appropriate relief, then the prosecutor stood up and said the state joined in the motion, dismissing all charges. It was all happening so fast that it didn't feel real. Nothing was sinking in.

"Mr. Cotton," the judge said, "the charges against you have been dropped. For the first time in a long time, you are walking out of here today a free man."

Tom turned and shook my hand, then Rich grabbed it. I know this more from watching the news coverage than actually having a memory of it. It felt kind of like falling back into the pond, like my ears were plugged up with water and everyone's voices were on the surface, distant. Diane told me she shrieked and threw her arms about my neck, hugging me for the first time in so many years. "Praise Jesus!" she said, before the judge told her to get out of his court with that.

The ADA, Rob Johnson, also turned to me and shook my hand, telling me he was sorry for everything I had been through on behalf of the state of North Carolina. Months later, I found out Mr. Johnson and the judge had made a special exception so I could simply walk out of the back of the courtroom that day, instead of returning to be deprocessed.

As Tom and Rich led me down the aisle, faces on both sides turned to look at me. Many people had tears in their eyes. They were all kind of a blur. People were reaching out to shake my hand, shake Tom's hand, shake Rich's hand. Even Phil Moseley was there in the back, with Dan Monroe, and I swear I saw a bit of moisture in the corner of ol' Phil's eye. Everyone seemed to be on their feet, and I couldn't believe I was heading for the back door to the courtroom, the one that led out to the hallway and the public restrooms and finally, the world outside. I walked numbly down the aisle, not sure how to take in what was happening. I had barely slept in two days. Before we opened that back door, Tom and Rich said they'd like to have a word and pulled me aside.

The three of us kind of huddled together. I don't think I had ever seen Rich in a suit, but he was dressed in gray, with a tie on and everything, and Tom looked like Matlock, a young Andy Griffith in a dark blue pinstriped suit.

"Ron, it is our great pleasure to end our representation of you today," said Rich. "We've been working on this case for three years, and we never dreamed it would turn out like this."

Tom continued. "We wanted to have a private moment with you just to reflect and be grateful for everything that's happened. In our careers, you don't see an injustice like this made right against all the odds."

I hugged them, thinking this moment had so much meaning. As much meaning as the moment I was sentenced. I tried to pinch myself to make sure it wasn't a dream.

I was really at a loss for words. "Thank you for the tremendous job you did for me. I know you didn't have to do any of it," I struggled. "I thank God that you took this case on. I don't know how I'll ever repay you."

"We don't want a dime for any of the work we've done, Ron. All we ask of you is to make the most of your freedom."

"Lead a productive life. That's the best payment we could ever ask for," Tom said.

"Ready?"

I nodded, and the three of us pushed open the courtroom door, where cameras flashed and people suddenly crowded around me. My sisters Tudy, Diane, and Pig, along with my nephews, gathered around me; my mom clutched my arm like she was never going to let go. We walked outside in the summer sun. Before I went off with them, I turned to shake Rich's hand again, like my soul was shaking his. Someone got a picture of that. It's up on my wall.

Walking away from the courthouse with my family, I looked up at the bright blue sky and said, "*Lord, where do I go from here?*"

CHAPTER 13

Jennifer

June 1995

MIKE GAULDIN AND ROB JOHNSON returned to my house in June. This time, we would not sit out on the deck off the kitchen and sip tea. The air was too thick, wrapping around you like a blanket the moment you stepped outside, so we stayed in where the air conditioner kept us cool. I have thought of Mike standing outside my door, sweating in the sticky June air, pausing for a minute before he knocked on the door. He had a job to do, yet he also knew he was about to completely shatter my world. He knew because it shook him in the same way; I could see it the moment he opened the door.

In the months since March, I had thought very little about the lab results. They were another formality, another desperate lawyer tactic: We all knew the results would show what I had known all along, what I had always known. It was Ronald Cotton who had broken into my apartment on July 29, 1984, held a knife to my throat, and raped me. It was Ronald Cotton who threatened to kill me, who had chased me through the rain that night while I fled for my life. It was Ronald Cotton's face I had been seeing in my nightmares for the last eleven years.

The neighbors' teenaged daughters took the triplets to the park earlier in the day, and Vinny stood next to me. Rob and Mike were very gentle when they delivered the news. The DNA found in Mary Reynolds's rape kit belonged to Bobby Leon Poole; it excluded Ronald Cotton. I shifted my hip to lean against the countertop, needed something solid to rest against because it felt like my insides were unraveling.

"What does that mean? How does it affect Jennifer?" Vinny asked, stoically. I wasn't capable of asking rational questions.

"It means we were wrong. Ronald Cotton was not your rapist," Mike said.

"As you know during the trial in 1987, the cases were consolidated because the state knew the perpetrator was the same man. Even though there was no DNA left to test in your kit," Rob explained, "we know that Bobby Poole assaulted you, too."

"But how do you know it's Bobby Poole?" Vinny asked.

"Mr. and Mrs. Cannino, Mike and Dexter Lowe went down to Central Prison to interview Bobby Poole."

"He knew details, Jennifer," Mike said, "about breaking the light at your back door, about holding a flashlight in Mary's face. What you both were wearing. Details only the person who attacked you could know."

"I personally stood outside in the prison exercise yard in the blazing sun just a few days ago when they were interviewing Poole. I told them to be sure. Poole denied everything for a long time, Mrs. Cannino," Rob said. "But when he was told the DNA evidence identified him, he finally confessed and provided details about the crimes that assured us he was the perpetrator."

Blood roared in my ears, an ocean of confusion crashing down on me, muffling their voices. Their faces searched mine, intent on discerning my emotional state.

". . . I can only imagine how difficult this must be for you . . ."

". . . This is not your fault . . ."

". . . We all made this mistake . . ."

I couldn't speak. I knew I had to keep it together in front of them, although it felt like everything I staked my life on—how I made sense of what happened to me—suddenly fell through a trap door. Silently, I berated myself. It meant I had screwed up. They had brought Bobby Poole into the courtroom during the second trial. How could I have been in the same room as my rapist and not recoil? I didn't even recognize him. Mike Gauldin was a first-rate cop who had risen through the ranks to captain from the young detective I met that awful night in the hospital, someone who had always treated me with dignity and respect. I had brought disgrace upon his investigation, and the whole Burlington Police Department. What did he think of me now?

"Jennifer, Ronald Cotton is going to be released from prison," Mike said.

"When?" Vinny asked.

"We're going to get him out of there as quickly as possible,"

Rob said. "Alamance County has no interest in keeping an innocent man behind bars. Ronald Cotton will not spend another night in prison that he doesn't have to."

Somehow I managed to mumble a thank you to the district attorney and to Mike for their professionalism. And they walked out my door to leave me in a world that suddenly made no sense at all.

• • •

For the first few days, I tried to keep patterns. I would get the triplets up, make their breakfast, load the dishwasher. Then I could move on to the routine afternoon tasks: vacuuming, making beds. As long as I stuck to my role of being a mom, I could hold myself together. Allowing myself to think outside of that was dangerous.

Mike Gauldin phoned me to let me know the date Ronald Cotton would be released, and I watched a brief news item about it on WXI channel 10. I have to say that the guilt over my part in robbing this man of so many years was not my first concern. Fear had opened up its maw and swallowed me whole. It was a fear even greater than what I felt in those early weeks before his arrest, because now I had children and a husband. I was waiting for Ronald Cotton—or his family—to come and exact revenge. It was only fair. I had wished for him to die violently and cruelly for what I believed he had done to me, so why wouldn't he want me to die for what I had taken from him?

On the outside, I seemed to be handling things. I had to: I was raising three young children who knew nothing about what had happened to their mother. But the shame and the anger sometimes suffocated me. My friend Andrea would come on long walks with me, listening to me as I cried and yelled. What was I supposed to do with the shame and the fear and the anger? I had no place to put it, and because I could not fall apart over it overtly, I fell apart over the most innocuous, unrelated things.

One evening as I was trying to get dinner on the table, I was taking hot rice out of the microwave in a glass dish. On autopilot, I used a damp dishtowel to hold it, and in seconds the heat shot through the towel to my hand. I let go of the dish, and it hit the open oven door next to me, sending rice and shattered glass all over the kitchen and in the oven. The kids were fighting over watching *Pinocchio,* and I started weeping hysterically. My husband came in and said, "It's OK, it's only rice. I'll help you clean it up."

"I don't want your help!" I yelled. "I'm doing it."

Brittany, Morgan, and Blake came in a few minutes later. "I'm hungry," they said. "When can we eat?" I would not let anyone sit down to eat until every last bit of rice was cleaned out of the oven, and I had swept up the glass on the floor.

In the fall when the kids started school, I went to the principal's office. He was a portly man with spectacles and receding hair. He listened kindly as I briefly explained what had happened, that this guy had come out of prison and I wanted the kids watched. The children were not to go with anybody, I told him. The principal took me very seriously and assured me he would meet with all three of their teachers.

I was so angry. I had been going through the world mostly

OK. I had volunteered for storytelling hour, had been the Girl Scout Brownie troop leader. My identity was Brittany, Morgan, and Blake's mom. People hadn't needed to know about my rape, and now I had to tell people not only was I a rape victim, but a rape victim with an extremely bad memory and someone had had to pay eleven years for that. I wondered how I could have been so stupid.

• • •

One weekend, when I was bringing the kids to visit my brother Joe, I knew we'd pass through Burlington. I called Mike Gauldin to see if he wanted to meet for coffee. We had breakfast at IHOP, and between meeting Mike and devouring their chocolate chip pancakes, the kids were rapt. He'd wanted to bring them something, but I guess all he could find were ballpoint pens. But ballpoint pens from "the police man" as they called him made every toy lying around our house pale in comparison. He even offered to give them a tour of the police station. They squealed in delight— "Can we mommy? Pleeeassse!" I called my brother to let him know we'd be later than expected.

Mike took the kids to the brand-new police building on Front Street. If it had been the same building I sat in all those years ago, I'm not sure I would have been able to walk in. He took the kids through every department. While they had their mug shots taken and were fingerprinted, Mike and I were able to talk a little. The case had haunted him the way it had haunted me, because Mike was a good cop. He told me he had been through the investigation file several times, trying to figure it all out, if there was a place where he had screwed up. He wanted to make sure it never happened again. Mike also told me officers reported seeing Ronald Cotton out and about, and that he seemed to be "at peace"; he really didn't think I was in any danger. Mike seemed more worried about what I was doing to myself.

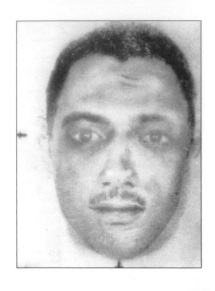

LEFT: Composite of the suspect created by Jennifer Thompson that was released to news media on July 29, 1984. (*Courtesy Burlington Police Department*)

BELOW RIGHT: The mug shot of Ronald Cotton that Jennifer Thompson selected during the photo identification session on July 31, 1984. (*Courtesy Burlington Police Department*)

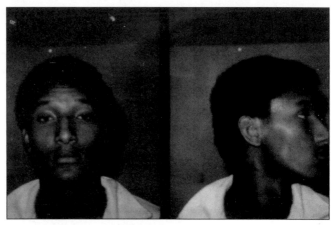

BELOW: Ronald Cotton's arrest mug shot, after going to the station voluntarily to "straighten things out." (*Courtesy Burlington Police Department*)

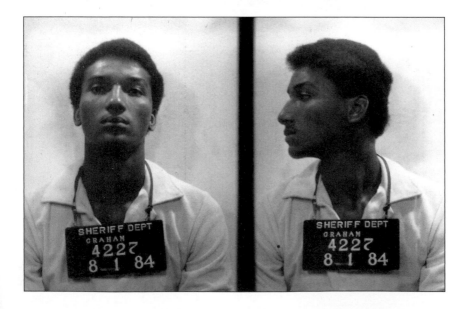

The physical lineup shown to both Jennifer Thompson and the second victim on August 8, 1984. Ronald Cotton was number five in the lineup. Jennifer picked number five after having some trouble deciding between four and five. The second victim identified number four as her assailant. Ron was the lone suspect in the lineup; all the others were stand-ins. (*Courtesy Burlington Police Department*)

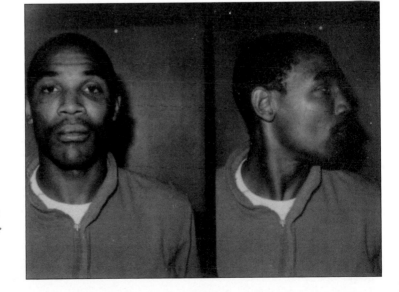

Mug shot of Bobby Leon Poole from his arrest. (*Courtesy Burlington Police Department*)

Polaroid of Ronald Cotton and Bobby Poole taken in Central Prison in September 1986 that Ron sent to his attorney. *"There is no doubt in my mind that Bobby Poole did the crime I'm serving time for. I work in the kitchen here with him. Mr. Moseley, as I've said before, Poole is the one. I've enclosed a picture of Poole and me. Maybe you could use it."* (Courtesy Ronald Cotton)

Alamance County Courthouse in Graham, North Carolina, where Ronald Cotton was tried and convicted in January 1985 and again in November 1987. *(Photo: Erin Torneo)*

Former Burlington Police Chief Mike Gauldin, who was the lead detective on Jennifer's case. *(Photo: Erin Torneo)*

Ronald Cotton's sister Tudy and his father, Jimmy, visiting him in prison, December 1991. *(Courtesy Tudy Bruce)*

Then Assistant District Attorney Rob Johnson (left) with Ronald Cotton's defense attorney, Rich Rosen, on June 30, 1995, the day Ron was exonerated. (*Photo: Joseph Rodriguez/*News & Record*)*

Ronald Cotton hugging his mother, Alameda Wheeler, after being freed. Ron's sister Diane and nephews B.J. and Brooks stand by. (*Photo: Joseph Rodriguez/*News & Record)

Ronald Cotton walks outside the courtroom, followed by his sisters Tudy, Theresa (Puddin'), Shelby, Diane, (not visible) Shelia (Pig), and his nephew Brooks. Shaking Rich Rosen's hand, Ron said, "It felt like my soul was shaking his." *(Photo: Joseph Rodriguez/News & Record)*

Ronald and Robbin Cotton congratulate Tom Lambeth (left) after he is sworn in as district court judge on August 30, 2007. *(Courtesy* The Alamance News*)*

With their respective daughters Raven and Brittany marching in front of them, Ronald Cotton and Jennifer Thompson-Cannino at the Community March for Justice for Troy Anthony Davis on October 13, 2007. *(Photo: Erin Torneo)*

At the end of the march, Ronald Cotton and Jennifer Thompson-Cannino speak to a crowd outside the Chatham County Courthouse in Savannah, Georgia. *(Photo: Erin Torneo)*

CHAPTER 14

Ronald

THE WEEKEND after my exoneration, I went with my family to watch the fireworks in Burlington City Park. It was the Fourth of July, 1995—Independence Day. Bobby Leon Poole had been indicted the day before for the rapes of Jennifer Thompson and Mary Reynolds. And while I finally had my innocence, I was a long way from independence.

My sister Tudy said I could stay with her and her sons, BJ and Brooks, until I got myself on my feet. Tudy's real name was Marietta, but we never called her that. Ever since she was a baby, she had round, rosy cheeks that we all used to love to pinch, saying "toot-toot"—and so she just became Tudy. She had an apartment in Gibsonville, North Carolina, and gave me the downstairs couch to sleep on. My nephews had just been babies when I went to prison, but now they were teenagers, and almost as tall as their mother. We razzed each other to the point where Tudy said one day that now she had "three sons." She was joking but, in a way, she was right: I was like a child, completely dependent on everyone else.

All those years with bars and razor wire around me—you're no better than a dog in a cage. After being locked up for so long, they just toss you out and expect you to deal with it. I had no money, and how could I explain on job applications where I had been for the last eleven years?

My younger brother Terry had come up from Fort Bragg to celebrate with us. I was real proud of him. The summer I was arrested, he had finished high school and was working in the mills, delivering yarn to the women working the machines. By the time my trial started, he had gone into the army. Now he was a drill sergeant working on his bachelor's degree. It was as if he saw my life going one way and just went the other direction.

As I made my way through the folding chairs and the people on blankets at the park, I felt the stares. So many people in the community had followed the case for years, had read the headlines calling me a "menace to society." Some glared at me suspiciously, as if I had just beaten a charge on some kind of technicality. There were others, though, who came up to me and shook my hand, others who had donated through churches to a fund Tom Lambeth had set up for me.

The sky above us lit up and exploded in colors. It was beautiful and frightening to me at the same time, how big and wide open the sky was, blank in the spaces between the fireworks. I was so hungry for life, but at the same time, it scared me. Some people come out after being in the system and they're just shell-shocked. They can't get themselves motivated to move forward. They're stuck, fear just grabbing at them; they just want to depend on others.

The first few months I was trapped in that shell, knocking on it, only cracking it, trying to come out. If I went out, I tried to have someone come with me. I was scared to go anywhere alone. I made sure I had receipts, made sure surveillance cameras at stores got good shots of me coming and going. I always wanted a witness, an alibi, for every minute.

I often went with Tudy to pick up my mom and take her to cash her social security checks. My mother was then living with her boyfriend in an apartment off Shop Road in Burlington. The stroke had left her weak on one side; one leg really bothered her, throwing her off balance. She was also starting to get spacey, like she had a touch of Alzheimer's. I didn't realize when we left court that the way she clutched my arm had more to do with her constant fear of falling. We'd go out walking and I'd have to say to her, "If you don't relax and loosen up, both of us will go down."

• • •

A few weeks after my release, Tom and I were invited to appear on the *Larry King Live* show out in Los Angeles. They would fly Tom and me out there and put us up. Did I want to go? Without a doubt, I told Tom yes. I had never been to Los Angeles before.

Tudy came with me to Greensboro to go shopping for a suit. All of my family had pitched in some cash for it; I was extremely touched. It was still very exciting for me to be wearing civilian instead of prison clothes, but this was my very first suit. It was light gray, with a double-breasted jacket. "You look good," Tudy told me, when I came out of the dressing room. "But you got to do something about that bushy hair; you look like you've been in a time warp." I laughed at myself in the mirror, looking almost like all the lawyers I had known over the years, except of course, for the two-inch Afro.

On the way home, I convinced Tudy to let me drive. She pulled over on a road that didn't have much traffic and I got behind the wheel. I put the car into drive and pulled out onto the open road in front of us. But I guess I was pretty rusty. As we rounded a corner, I was too fast with the speed and cut the turn too short and plowed us right into a curb. Tudy screamed as the car hit the curb with a thud and then jumped it. I put the car into park.

"Ron, you got to slow down! Let me drive until you practice some more," Tudy said.

"C'mon Toot, let me drive home. I've got to do it, I've got to figure it out. I'll go slow, I promise," I told her. She looked at me as skeptically as she used to back when we were small. She was a bit of a tomboy growing up; she'd follow me around and I'd convince her to do things she didn't really want to do. One time when we had been out in the woods, I had told her, "Jump across! Just swing on the vine." She had grabbed hold of the Tarzan vine and jumped to swing across the creek, but she only made it about halfway across and fell on her behind, right in the muddy creek bed.

"Just don't mess up my car," she said.

She let me drive the rest of the way back to her place, but she braced herself with a hand on the dashboard and closed her eyes every time we got near a turn.

Tudy's neighbor was dating a barber who had a chair in Burlington, so I called him up one day to make an appointment. His name was Lonnie, and it turned out we had gone to school together, Elon Elementary and Elon Middle School all the way up to Western

High School before I dropped out. He read a lot about me in the papers, he said. "I feel very privileged to be the first one to cut your hair since you come out. You think it'll be a scene?" I told him no, I didn't think that my getting a haircut was going to be any kind of news. Some people thought it was strange for me to go back to the community where I had been convicted—I either got dirty looks or people acted like I was a celebrity. Either way, everyone always seemed to know me.

With my new haircut and new suit, I boarded a plane for Los Angeles. Buckling myself in next to Tom, I couldn't help but think of the time I had flown on Express One out to Tennessee and how I never could have imagined this present journey in my wildest dreams. Tom and I talked most of the six hour trip. We didn't know much about each other personally before, on account of Tom and Rich's being so busy with my case and all. I learned he had grown up right in Burlington, too. He even owned an ice-cream shop. Tom had gone to law school at UNC–Chapel Hill, where Rich Rosen had been one of his professors. "He's one of my heroes," Tom said. I told him I knew exactly what he meant; he and Rich were both heroes to me. Tom asked me a lot about myself, how I'd come up, and how I was doing.

"To be real honest with you, I need a job," I said to him. "I hate feeling like I'm still a burden on my family. I want to get my life started, but I can't without any money. I don't even have a driver's license anymore. I have to take the test all over again."

"If I can help you find a job, I will. I promise. Let me see what I can do when we get home. Now, I want to share some good news with you."

"What is it?"

"The governor is going to sign a pardon of innocence. I'm going to announce it on the *Larry King* show."

"What does that mean?"

"It means the highest official in the state of North Carolina is formally recognizing that you were innocent of all charges for which you served time. It's important for the public to know that, people who don't quite understand yet what DNA tests mean."

DNA was just beginning to be big news because of the O. J. Simpson trial. At the mall, I had joined people crowding around the TVs in Sears the day the verdict came out. When they said, "not guilty," everyone had gasped. Part of the *Larry King Live* show was about making people understand how DNA was being used in trials.

I was so nervous being on television that behind the desk in the *Larry King* studio, I had a balled-up paper towel in my swampy hands, trying to keep them dry. I tried to stay collected, sitting beside Tom, who wore a black suit with a white shirt. At every commercial break, a girl came over to put more makeup on us. She only put a little bit on my forehead, but she really pounded the makeup on Tom. Larry King told me to call him Larry, not "sir." "It throws me," he said, but I noticed Tom also kept calling him "sir." I guess he was nervous, too.

The assistant district attorney who had been at my exoneration was patched through from Raleigh with Rich Rosen. I could see them on a TV monitor in the background.

They talked a lot about DNA, how DNA was even better than eyewitness identification because people can make mistakes. Larry King wanted to know about the two women who made those mistakes. Rob Johnson talked about the fact that there was a "total absence of malice"—that's what he called it—on the part of the victims. Of course Larry King asked me the question everybody always wanted to ask: "And you're not angry, right?"

It was hard to put it into words, especially sweating there on live television, that I had had eleven years to think about what had happened to me, years in prison where I made a decision to let go of the anger and frustration. Since I had gotten out, I went twice a week to Hester Grove Baptist Church, and came to feel that God had given me a second chance at life, a chance to really make something of myself and I could only go forward. Anger would have just kept me stuck, as if I'd never left prison. But I did have a lot of questions I wondered if I'd ever have answers to. I wanted to know why: Why had Jennifer Thompson thought it was me? I could not express it, so all I said to Larry King was "No, I'm not angry."

I listened as Rob spoke about how she was going through a lot of feelings, a lot of emotions. Then Rob pointed out that all three of us had been victims of the same rapist, in a way.

At a certain point in the show, Larry King took callers. Some man actually called from Burlington, North Carolina, who said it was just a coincidence he was from there, that he didn't know any of us personally. He had read an article in the paper that talked about the fact that if it had been the seventies, I could have received the death penalty for the crimes, and could have been executed before the system figured out the mistake.

"Must be scary to think you could have been executed," Larry King said to me.

I thought of many of the guys I met at Central Prison once I started working on the kitchen crew, guys who were on death row, no hope left. I don't know how it would have all turned out if I had been in their shoes. I only knew there were more men inside who were innocent, and I wondered if they'd ever get their chance to prove it.

Another caller asked if I received training or education in prison, and Larry King wanted to know if I was working.

"No, sir," I told him.

"Well, what kind of work do you want to do?"

"Anything to start out, doesn't have to be any certain type of job, just a job," I said.

"But is there something special you want to do?"

"A job is a job," I said.

. . .

Soon after we returned to North Carolina, Tom made good on his word. That's the thing about Tom: he's just that kind of guy you can always count on. "I called a friend of mine, Dr. James Powell—he's head of LabCorp—and let him know what a good kid you are and asked if there might be any openings," Tom told me on the phone. "He's delighted to help, wants you to call the number I'm about to give you and you can go on in for an interview."

At the end of the summer, I started working for LabCorp in downtown Burlington. The funny thing was that LabCorp was the same company that had tested my DNA. It wasn't the same office—that had been the Raleigh branch—but, still. The job was an important first step in my trying to start my life again. I worked in shipping and receiving, checking in packages drivers came to unload at the loading dock. I'd come down with a clipboard and check to make sure the purchase order numbers lined up, then I punched them into a computer that would tell me what individual was expecting what package. Then I'd help deliver them in a cart. I got to meet a lot of people working at the company that way. That's how I met Robbin.

Robbin worked in the cyto prep department. I thought she looked a little like that actress Jada Pinkett: she was a small woman with long, curly, corkscrew hair and glasses, and she acted tough as nails. Turns out we had met years before, although I didn't really recall it. She knew one of my sisters, and had come up in the Burlington area herself. When we ran into each other in the break room, she said, "I read the stories about you in the newspaper a long time ago. And I never thought it could be you." She reminded me we had met briefly before. "Whenever I saw you on the street, you were always so polite; you'd smile and say hello. I just knew you couldn't have done what they said."

Since my release, magazines and newspapers were always calling me up, asking me questions. The thing I liked about Robbin was she never asked me questions. We took to having lunch together, and if I wanted to talk, she would listen. If I did talk about the things that happened, Robbin, for all her toughness, would usually end up with waterworks. Since being convicted—even wrongly— of rape, I felt strange around women. I was unsure, after all those years, how to approach them, move forward. I didn't want to do the wrong thing or say the wrong thing that would push someone away. Luckily for me, Robbin was very patient, and that's what I needed.

"Why are you crying?" I said to her one day, as we were getting ready to head back to work.

"You remind me of an abused kid I used to know. I can't imagine what it was like to try to tell someone for all those years that you didn't do it and nobody's hearing you. You're innocent and nobody listens to anything that you say," she cried. "Ron, I'm so sorry that you went through that. It's not fair for anybody to go through what you did."

I hugged her then, and I realized we were both starting to really care for each other.

I was studying the driver's manual again, because I had to apply for a new driver's license after all these years and take the road test again. Robbin would quiz me sometimes. She also took me out driving in her teal green Honda Accord, pointing out places that I had forgotten. It was strange to be back at home but to constantly feel lost while driving around. It made me realize how long I had been gone. When we went up on the interstate, I would get queasy in the passenger seat with all the cars flying by. As cars would approach the passenger's side in another lane, I'd jerk, sure they were going to hit us. I was so used to being transported—with bars on the window—when I couldn't see a lot and people couldn't see me. It was even harder to learn to drive on my own—to trust all the freedom that I suddenly had.

· · ·

My father had been in a rest home, and I wasn't sure where it was. One Sunday, Robbin picked me up.

"I've got a surprise for you," she said, when I got in the car.

"Oh, yeah? Where're we going?"

"We're going to visit your daddy," she said.

"Robbin, you know where it is? You know how to get there?" It had been years since I had seen my father, although I thought all the time of how important his words had been to me, getting through it all the right way and not giving up hope.

"Not really, but we'll find it," she said.

After some wrong turns down long country roads, we found my daddy's nursing home in Hillsborough. He had had a stroke years ago, and now he also had colon cancer. He could no longer walk on his own, and he needed help to go to the bathroom.

We found him sitting in his wheelchair by a window.

"Dad," I said.

He turned, like he couldn't believe his ears.

"Son," he said. "You're home."

I knelt down by him and squeezed him hard. My big, tough father seemed to be shrunken down to a bag of bird bones. He was so happy to see me that tears just fell out of his eyes.

"I'm so glad you're out," he said. "I told you the good Lord was going to shine the light on the truth, didn't I?"

He took Robbin's hand as I introduced her. She bent down to kiss him on the cheek.

"Nice to meet you, young lady," he said.

We spent the rest of the afternoon talking, about nothing and everything. Every once in a while my father would just stop and look at me as if he couldn't believe his eyes. I told my father I could bring him some things if he wanted, like a radio.

"I had a radio, but Nate," he nodded in the direction of his roommate's bed, "that's my roommate. That son of a bitch is crazy—excuse my language, young lady—he's always stealing my belongings!

"There is something I'd really like . . ." he continued, and then tried to sweet-talk Robbin into buying him some chips from a vending machine down the hall.

"Dad," I said, "you got high-blood pressure; you know that stuff's no good for you."

He winked at Robbin. "Don't you believe him, ain't nothing that can hurt me now."

After that, Robbin came with me every Sunday to visit him, and once I got my license, I would try to borrow a car and get out and see him when I could. I loved just driving around, listening to the radio and singing along with it. But even with my own license, I was still having a hard time figuring out where I was going. Once, I drove twenty-five miles out of my way trying to get to a bowling alley, and eventually I had to pull over and call Robbin. "I'm lost," I told her.

• • •

Tom told me the governor's pardon of innocence made me eligible for a state statute that would give me some compensation for the years I had been wrongfully incarcerated. I remember when Tom had talked about it on *Larry King Live,* and how Tom had kept trying to explain the amount and Larry kept getting it wrong. When Tom said $500 per year, Larry thought he said $500 a month. Then Tom said there was a maximum of $5,000, and Larry thought Tom meant I'd get $5,000 a year. Finally, Tom cleared it up for him: For eleven years of my life, I could get $5,000 from the State of North Carolina. Tom and Rich said they were trying to find a legislator to support a new bill, to change the money. I guess North Carolina had never had anyone like me to deal with. I was the first person in the state to be exonerated by DNA. Everybody thought $5,000 was so little, but any amount of money would have helped Robbin and me get our lives together. We both worked long hours trying to make ends meet.

I had started taking some classes at the Alamance Community College, working toward my GED. I enjoyed meeting people, but it got really hectic trying to study and make enough money. Eventually, I had to make a decision between school and making some money for myself.

I took a second job at a restaurant called the Golden Corral. My shift at LabCorp ended at three o'clock, and I'd head over to Golden Corral and work until about ten at night. Golden Corral had a baking area out in the open, so kids would wander up and watch pizza dough getting tossed. I liked it because you could watch people coming and going. One evening, I was measuring out yeast for the yeast rolls when I noticed Detective Lowe come in to be seated with his wife. When he saw me, he nodded and headed over.

He stuck out his hand for me to shake. "I just wanted to tell you I'm sorry about everything," he said.

I nodded.

"Everyone is. Jennifer, too."

I wondered, if she was really sorry, why didn't she tell me herself?

"We were just doing our jobs, you know?"

"Yeah," I said, getting back to my job.

• • •

After saving up enough money, Robbin and I decided to move in together. A lot of people thought we were moving fast, but I didn't have time to waste. It felt good to be in love, to be loved again after all that time. We found an apartment on Holly Street in Burlington. For a while, all we really had was a bed to sleep on.

Slowly, we began to get other stuff. My mom gave us some living room furniture she didn't want anymore and then we saved up some money to buy kitchen things. It was the first place I'd ever had on my own. One night, I made her a steak dinner and said, "Let's get married."

Robbin and I got married on December 21, 1996, the day I turned thirty-five, in her grandma's house—Pastor Onslow Holt officiated. The following week, we were going to have a big party at a restaurant in downtown Burlington called the Occasion. I showered the morning of the reception, excited to see all my family and friends—Tom Lambeth was coming, too—all the people who had stood by me, and celebrate. But when I got out of the shower, I saw Robbin sitting on the bed by the phone, looking pale.

"C'mere a minute," she said, patting the bed next to her. "I need to talk to you."

I sat down beside her.

"Ron, Tudy just called. Daddy passed," she said.

I looked at her, with more hurt in my eyes than I knew what to do with. *How much more am I going to have to go through?* I thought. I couldn't believe after so many years being apart that now my father was dead. I wanted him to see me make something of myself, I wanted to make him proud. Robbin held my hand and cried with me, and when I felt like I had no more tears in me, we got ready for our wedding reception.

At the party, I felt very happy and very sad at the same time. My mom also sat in her chair most of the night, although when she was younger she would have been up dancing. I sat down next to her and kissed her cheek. She looked at me.

"When the good Lord dials your number, it's time to go," she said. "I know he wasn't always the father you wanted him to be, but he was there in time of need. He was always running around telling people, 'Ron's innocent. I know he is.' He had no doubt. Not for a minute. He was always proud of you, even while you were incarcerated. Damn proud."

CHAPTER 15

Jennifer

ON A TRIP to the outer banks, I made a deal with the kids: If they behaved, we could stop at McDonald's. The kids were collecting the Batman toys that came with the Happy Meals. Unfortunately for me, my six-year-olds could only hold out so long, and I pulled off the freeway in Graham, just blocks from the courthouse where my rape trials had been. I was standing in line with the kids, and happened to turn around. I found myself looking into the blue eyes of Phil Moseley. Instinctively, I shrank from him.

"Hi," he said, tentatively. "I don't know if you remember me—"

"I know who you are, Phil Moseley," I said.

"I just want you to know," he said, "that despite all the trials, I am so sorry for what happened to you back then."

"Thank you," I said tightly, wanting the conversation to end and wishing I could run out of there. I felt so ashamed, and guilty.

"You are in my prayers all the time."

I blinked at him, stunned, and then turned back around. I could scarcely breathe, because I was fighting tears and I could not start crying in front of my kids. All these years, I had thought of Phil Moseley as a hideous bastard. I hated him as I had hated Ronald Cotton. His kindness was simply too much to bear.

· · ·

In 1996, a producer named Ben Loeterman phoned me about doing a story for *Frontline* on PBS. It was going to be a story about how eyewitnesses can make mistakes. My first instinct was, no way. Why would I want to go on national TV and admit that I had picked the wrong guy not once, but twice?

I weighed the pros and cons with Mike Gauldin and Vinny. I had spent so many years protected by law from the public's knowing my name, struggling to keep separate my roles of mother, witness, and victim. While Mike and Vinny both worried about the effects of me reliving it all on camera, in the end I decided I needed to do it. It was the beginning of a shift in me—a shift that really began when I found myself face to face with Phil Moseley, unable to justify the hatred I had for him. The mistake I made affected so many lives, and I still had so many questions about how it could have happened. Before it happened to me, I didn't think a mistake like this was even possible.

And no matter what the science told me, I saw the face of Ronald Cotton in my memories. The producer told me it would help me understand why my memory had done that—why my mind had made it so Bobby Poole, my rapist, became unrecognizable to me three years after my assault. I knew it was risky to show my face on TV, but there was no longer any way I could pretend that I had put the rape behind me. Finally, I agreed on the condition that I have no contact with Ronald Cotton, whom they were also asking to participate. During the month or so of filming, the crew would often tell me that Ronald Cotton was a really wonderful guy, that he wasn't angry at all.

"What Jennifer Saw" aired in February 1997, but I couldn't watch the broadcast. I had my husband tape it so I could watch it by myself. I wasn't sure how I'd react, seeing myself describe details of my rape on camera, or seeing Ronald Cotton's face and hearing his voice. The morning after it aired, when I had the house to myself, I put in the tape and watched it with my dog Bingo lying at my feet.

At the end of the film, Ronald Cotton told the interviewer that he wondered why he had never heard from me.

"I would like to hear what she has to say—in her own words—to me," he said.

When the film finished, the screen went to static. I put it on mute and just sobbed while the black and white blizzard raged onscreen.

Ron's words reverberated through my head: "I would like to hear what she has to say—in her own words—to me."

I looked around the den, at the photos of my three children smiling back at me from the walls, and a picture of Vinny and me on our wedding day. Eleven years. How do eleven years pass when you are locked up for a crime you didn't commit? I couldn't begin to imagine. For me, they were eleven years measured in birthdays, first days of school, Christmas mornings.

Ronald Cotton and I were exactly the same age, and he had had none of those things because I'd picked him. He'd lost eleven years of time with his family, eleven years of falling in love, getting married, having kids. He looked forlorn on the television, hurt and bewildered. The guilt suffocated me.

I started straightening up the house. I cooked and cleaned and organized so I would stop crying. When I finished the dishes, I wiped my hands on the dish towel and took a deep breath. I picked up the phone.

"Captain Gauldin's office," his secretary answered.

"May I speak with Captain Gauldin, please?"

"Who's calling please?"

"Jennifer Thompson-Cannino."

"One moment."

As I was being patched through, I curled the phone cord tightly around a finger. I couldn't believe what I was about to do, but my loudly drumming heart marched me forward. After a few minutes, he picked up the phone.

"Jennifer! What a nice surprise," he said. "Did you watch the show?"

Mike had participated, as well as Phil Moseley.

"I did," I said.

"How are you?" he asked.

"Um, I'm calling to ask you, well, I need to ask you a favor—"

"I know what you're going to say," he interrupted, catching me off guard.

"You do?"

"Yeah. You want to meet Ron, don't you?"

"Yes," I said, exhaling with relief. "Can you help?"

"Absolutely. Let me make a few calls."

"Thanks, Mike."

• • •

After watching me suffer so much in the two years since Ronald Cotton's release, Vinny knew I had not come to my decision hastily. He supported it, because he thought it might help me. "You've got to do something," he said, "you can't go on like this."

My sister Janet, however, was completely against the idea. She had already been very concerned about my decision to be public. She thought there was too much information out there about me, and she feared for the kids.

"He was no choirboy, you know that. You know he didn't live a right life before. You probably did him a service, he'd have probably wound up in jail anyway."

"You don't know that," I said. "We don't really know who he is. I just know that I took him away from his family for so many years, it's not right."

"You don't owe him anything, Jennifer, it was a mistake."

"Please just try to understand that I have to do this," I said to her.

"Well, I know you're just going to do whatever you set your mind to do, but that doesn't mean I have to be happy about it."

My parents' reaction was slightly less severe. We had gone for coffee at The Dessertery in Winston-Salem. They still hadn't watched the PBS film, something I hoped they would do because it might give us the chance, after all these years, to talk about it openly. When I told them I had made a decision to go and meet Ronald Cotton, my mother looked down into her coffee. My father patted me on the knee, and said, "Well, honey, if that'll make you feel better," before changing the subject.

In the parking lot, we hugged good-bye, then we turned to get into our respective cars. My father stopped me as I was getting in and said, "I just wanna caution you, just know that every time you lift the lid off the garbage can, it's gonna stink."

CHAPTER 16

Ronald

WHEN TOM CALLED ME up and said that Jennifer Thompson wanted to meet me, it didn't even take a blink of an eye for me to decide.

"For real?" I said. "Yeah. I'd be glad to."

But when I told Robbin I was going to meet Jennifer, she was furious.

"What could she possibly want from you now?" she said.

"Robbin, I want to do this," I told her. When I had watched the PBS movie and heard Jennifer Thompson say she knew I didn't do it, but that she still saw my face, she might as well have pushed a knife into my heart. It hurt. I needed to ask her why. What was it about me that made her think it was me? If she met me, would she be able to see I wasn't a monster?

Everything in Robbin just hardened. We argued back and

forth on it for a week. She was real protective of me and I can't blame her for that.

"She went on with her life, and now you're trying to go on with yours and what is she trying to do? Mess with it again? It's not fair. You don't owe her anything," Robbin said.

"Why are you so angry about this?" I said.

"Because you aren't angry enough," she said.

I had had eleven years to deal with everything, but for Robbin, all of this was still new.

"What good is anger going to do me?"

"Why do you always have to make it OK for everybody else? I know you're always telling everyone you're fine. You don't want anyone's pity. Do you know how hard it is, to lie by your side night after night and watch you flinch in your sleep, yelling 'No! No! No!'" she cried.

The fighting wore me down. Finally I said to her, "Robbin, I'm going with or without you."

The date had been set for April 4, 1997, and just a few days before, Robbin went to speak to her minister and her mother about it. When she returned she said to me, "It's not fair for me to not want you to go. You're the one who needs to be able to put this stuff to rest, to find peace if you can."

And in the end, Robbin agreed to come with me, but the whole thing just made her suspicious. We drove over to Tom's office that day so we could all go together. The location of the meeting was kind of hush-hush because no one wanted it leaked to the media. No one knew what was going to happen, and I guess we all had had enough cameras in our faces. Tom explained that the assistant district attorney, Rob Johnson, was a deacon at the

First Baptist Church of Elon College and his pastor suggested we all meet there.

The church was set back some from the road. It was all brick with a stained-glass window in the front, a picture of a flying dove. Service was over for the day; there were only a few cars there in the parking lot.

Gauldin met Tom and me in the doorway. Instantly, I flashed back to the day I'd walked into the police station and laid eyes on Gauldin for the first time. Since my release, I had seen him and Lowe around town, and almost every time they apologized to me. "It's good to see you, Ron. How're you doing?" Gauldin said to me.

"I can't really complain. I'm doing well."

I stepped inside with Robbin and Tom. Waiting just around the corner in the hallway was Jennifer Thompson and her husband, and Rob Johnson, the prosecutor who'd dismissed all the charges against me. We all stood there for a moment, just looking at one another. In the police department, and in the courtroom, there had always been sides. Now here we were, nothing to separate us.

Someone introduced Jennifer Thompson and me, which was kind of funny when you think about it. We had known each other's names for a long time. Even if we had never met again, or never saw each other, I would have remembered Jennifer Thompson's name for the rest of my life, just as I'm sure she would have remembered mine.

She asked to speak with Robbin and me privately, so with her husband, a guy named Vinny, we went into the pastor's study. It was a small, wood-paneled room with a big desk in it, and a couch. Everyone else waited in the hallway. I could tell Gauldin wasn't so sure about leaving Jennifer alone, but she asked him and everyone else to stay out. So Tom and Mike had no choice but to sit out in the hallway.

Jennifer had on a long jean dress. Her hair was still blond and cut shorter than it had been all those years ago. We had both been so much younger then. She looked very nervous. I think it was kind of a shock, our being face to face. We had never actually been that close to each other. Jennifer looked like she wasn't sure what to say or do. She looked down at the ground, then up at Robbin and then at me.

She was very emotional already. I could see she was still stuck in all that had happened to her, and probably always would be. It reminded me of a something Robbin said a lot, about the look I sometimes got. "As close as we are Ron, I can't reach you when you go there," she'd say to me.

"Mr. Cotton. I don't even know what to call you. Ron? Ronald? Mr. Cotton? If I spent the rest of my life telling you how sorry I am, it wouldn't come close to how I feel," Jennifer said. "Can you ever forgive me?"

Sometimes people don't have to say a thing. If you look directly into their eyes, it's all there. People's eyes talk. I learned to read people like that when I was in prison. So it was good to be there, to hear her and see the expressions on her face. I could see that she was truly sorry. It was plain as day: If she could've gone back and turned the hands of time to change what happened, she would have.

"I forgive you," I told her. "I'm not angry at you. I don't want you to spend the rest of your life looking over your shoulder, thinking I'm out to get you, or harm your family. If you look, I'm not going to be there. All I want is for us all to go on and have a happy life."

Jennifer looked at me, speechless. Her whole face trembled and she got tears in her brown eyes. I could see there was pain, a lot of pain that she was trying to let go. For the first time, in so many years, I didn't see the hate in her eyes. She didn't look at me and see the man who had hurt her, the man she wanted dead, she saw *me*. I didn't even think about it until after the fact, but I reached for her hands and all of a sudden, we were standing there, hugging. The next thing I knew, Robbin, Mrs. Ball Breaker herself, was bawling, too. And before I even realized it, tears fell from my eyes.

• • •

Jennifer asked me questions about life in prison, how I had survived. She also asked me how my life had been since I had gotten out, how I was getting along.

"I had to believe God had a plan," I said, "and that this miscarriage of justice would one day be revealed. I used to read the Book of Psalms a lot."

"Did you know Bobby Poole?" she asked me.

I could see her wince at his name, and the memories of what he had done.

"I met him in prison. I had known some of his family, coming up in the area, but I didn't know him," I paused, wishing I could give her more answers. "It's true what Rob Johnson said: We were both his victims."

Robbin looked at me and I knew she needed to say something. She kept quiet and let me say what I needed to say. That couldn't have been easy. I nodded that it was OK for her.

"Jennifer, I have a lot of anger with you. But this hurt you see being released, you need to see it. Ronald's a good man. There aren't many men that could fill his shoes."

Robbin then asked if she could talk to Jennifer alone. Jennifer agreed to do it, so her husband and I went into the next room. Mike Gauldin and Tom jumped up when we left the room. It felt to me like no time had gone by, but I guess to them it felt like hours. "Everything going all right in there?" Tom asked.

"Yeah, my wife just wanted to talk to Jennifer alone."

Mike Gauldin and Tom nodded, and Vinny and I took seats next to them. The four of us guys just shrugged at each other and wondered what the heck Robbin and Jennifer could be saying to each other.

CHAPTER 17

Jennifer

WHEN ROBBIN COTTON asked to speak with me alone, I knew I had to oblige, however uncomfortable it made me. Her anger seemed packed up like a closed jack-in-the-box, ready to spring as soon as there was an opening. For a moment, after Ronald and Vinny stepped out of the study, I honestly wondered if she was going to slug me.

Peering through the blinds of the pastor's study window earlier in the day, I had watched their truck pull into the parking lot. I held Vinny's hand, wondering if I was stupid or brave. In shock, I let go of Vinny's hand when Ronald got out of his truck and walked around to open the door for his wife. As he stood beside Robbin, I noticed how tall he was and flashed back to the kinesthetic memory of my body, standing in the dark hallway of my apartment the night I was attacked next to the man who threatened to kill me. My rapist had not been that tall. It was the first of many surprises. Robbin was another one, of course. I simply had no idea I would be facing not only Ronald, but his wife, too.

But I knew it was Robbin's right to be there. So I stood there, smoothing my hands on my dress and readying myself for whatever she felt like she had to do.

"Jennifer, this mistake you made. If you ever got to know Ron, you would know just how wrong you were. Ron is probably one of the most loving people you will ever meet in your life. I'm still so angry about this. You need to know that now," she said.

"Mrs. Cotton—"

"Robbin."

"Robbin, I am so sorry. I know I was so wrong."

"I know you went through something awful, but I just don't see how you could think that about him. What took you so long to come forward?" she demanded.

"When he first got out, the police advised me not to do anything. They said it was too risky. But I thought about him every day." I remembered what my minister said to me when I went to see him, trying to summon my courage. "I don't know what I'm doing, how do I do this?" I had asked him. He had told me, "You will just know. The words will come to you, ask God and he will be your words." But the words coming to me were obscenely inadequate. *Help me out here, God,* I thought.

Fortunately for both of us, Ron knocked on the door then and came in. He looked at me and looked at Robbin and said gently to his wife, "Are you OK?"

"Ron, I don't know if I'll ever be OK with this. Because she hurt you so bad and I can't believe anybody would ever hurt you that bad," Robbin said, crying.

Another thing that stunned me: how gentle and soft-spoken Ronald Cotton was, nothing like the menacing voice I could still hear hissing in my mind, the voice I had associated with his image for so long. And I had certainly never imagined that he would stand before me and say, "I forgive you," just that easily and that simply. He was free, I realized, truly free.

By the time we made our way outside to the parking lot, twilight was deepening around us. Mike and Tom, wet-eyed themselves, stood off to the side to give us a moment to say good-bye before we went our separate ways.

"It's going to be all right," Ron said, taking Robbin, who was still sobbing, into his arms. Then he reached out and Vinny and I ended up in his embrace. What a foursome. Sure, he was a very tall man. But it was an inner strength he had that must've allowed him to survive all those years in prison, to wait for the truth to come out. He seemed to be holding us all up.

. . .

Mike drove us back, and as we passed the familiar streets of Burlington and Elon—the church must have been just a couple of miles from where I had been raped—I felt my anger with the community begin to drain away. Because this small town, where things were greening already and eager to bloom after winter, this town was also Mike Gauldin, Dexter Lowe, Rob Johnson, and Tom Lambeth who had gone far beyond their job descriptions as police officers, defense attorneys, and prosecutors to help make something right.

We had dropped off the kids with Mike's secretary earlier in the day. They had been told that Mommy had an important meeting, but they didn't really care once they heard they were going to get to hang out in the police station. Morgan, Brittany, and Blake came down to meet us with their arms full of stickers, coloring books, toy badges, and teddy bears. Morgan, always the protective one, said, "Mommy, can we come back again? But next time don't let Blake eat so many doughnuts. He got a stomachache."

They did not notice how quiet the adults were when we went out to dinner; Mike accompanied us. We had to be careful about talking around the kids, but we all kept looking at one another, trying to process what had just happened. All I could think was: *Had I really just been in the arms of the man I had accused of raping me?*

• • •

A few weeks later, Mike called to tell me that Tom Lambeth, Ronald's attorney, was working on getting a bill passed that would increase the amount of money Ronald could get for every year he had spent in prison. "Right now, he's only going to get about five thousand dollars," Mike said. I was shocked. Tom had asked for letters of support. Mike had written one, he said. Would I be interested in writing one, too? "Of course," I told him. It was the least I could do. Immediately, I sat down at my kitchen table with a yellow legal pad and pen:

April 16, 1997

To the attention of Joe Hackney
           Dennis Reynolds
           Wayne Goodwin
Dear sirs:
Almost thirteen years ago my world was turned upside down by a brutal and violent attack against my body, my soul, and

my spirit. I survived and swore that my attacker would be punished and spend the rest of his life in what I hoped would be full of fear and regrets. I did what I thought was the right thing.

In cooperation with the authorities, I picked out a man named Ronald Cotton. I testified in a court of law that this was the man who raped me. "That's the man," I said, "he's the one who raped me."

Eleven years later, I found out that the face I had grown to fear, the name I had grown to loathe, was the wrong man. I would now begin a new journey, this one filled with fear and regrets, the two things I wished for Mr. Cotton.

It is now clear to me that we were and are victims of the same man, Bobby Leon Poole. I ask you to stop, close your eyes, open your hearts, and imagine what it must have been like for Ronald Cotton. An innocent man, looking at spending his entire life behind bars for a crime he did not commit. Days turn into months, months turn into years. Birthdays, holidays, and celebrations are gone forever. He is no longer twenty-two years old but thirty-three and suddenly told, "You are a free man."

His world has been turned upside down by a brutal and violent attack against his body, his soul, and his spirit. I know his pain all too well. Can you give him back his years, that life, those moments? No. But we can try to make his new life, his future, and his dreams easier and real. Please consider his requests and others that are in the same situation as Mr. Cotton. He is an extraordinary man, with extraordinary potential. As a society, let's not make another mistake!

Sincerely,
Jennifer Thompson

• • •

I don't think, until I stood weak-kneed in front of Ronald, that I had any idea what forgiveness was, nor how powerful it could be. Ronald gave me something that eluded me in the thirteen years since that sweltering summer night: the gift of forgiveness—not because I deserved it, but because that's what grace is about. It was the real beginning of my journey back.

Forgiveness is tricky. People think when you forgive someone, you excuse what he did. That's not what it is. It's about power and letting go. Forgiveness certainly didn't come to me as easily as it did for Ronald, but I realized Bobby Poole still had a hold on me after all these years and that the anger that lived in me had completely changed the way I looked at the world, at what was possible.

If Ronald had forgiven me so gracefully, so completely, could I forgive the man who had hurt us both? That day we met in church, I asked Ronald if he had forgiven Bobby Poole.

"I don't really feel like I have to," he'd said. "I heard he's dying, from cancer or something. So if not for the DNA he would have gone to his death, still not admitting anything. But I'm already past it, and it's not going to do anything for me."

For years I had harbored anger—misdirected of course—anger that kept me caged in fear, judging Ronald even after his innocence, judging Phil Moseley as less than human. I wanted to be as open in my heart as Ronald had been, to stand before me and forgive me. I needed to forgive Bobby Poole, not for his sake, but for mine.

I called Mike Gauldin up and asked if he thought meeting Bobby Poole was a possibility.

"You can certainly request it, but honestly, I don't think your chances are good. People like him are cowards, Jennifer. I'll get you the address to write him, but don't get your hopes up."

Even if Bobby Poole was a coward, I knew that I needed to show him he had not destroyed me that night. It was my way of letting it go, something I never could have done if I hadn't met Ronald Cotton. On the very same yellow pad I used to write a letter in support of Ronald, I wrote a letter to my rapist.

April 18, 1997

Dear Mr. Poole:

Thirteen years ago you broke into my world uninvited, and stole from me items more precious than gold. You raped my body, devastated my soul, and shattered my spirit. I have gone through many stages of healing over these years and this is my final stage.

It has come to my attention that you have cancer and your health is not good. So I am writing requesting to see you. For a third of my life, memories, questions, and fear have haunted me. I need to face the person responsible for putting them there.

I am not interested in standing in judgment of you because that day is coming very quickly for you and it is not for me to do. However, I do want to look into your eyes so I can put to rest the many questions I have had for so long.

I faced you with courage and bravery on that July night; you never asked my permission. Now I ask you to face me, but I am asking for yours. Please reply as soon as possible.

Sincerely,
Jennifer Thompson

. . .

As Mike predicted, my letter to Bobby Poole went unanswered. But something else surprising happened: Ronald Cotton and I began to talk. At first we talked because we were dealing with interview requests. I always called Ronald to see if he might be able to come, too.

We were friendly with each other, exchanging small talk initially. But while reporters would check their notes and photographers would set up, we found time to learn about each other's lives. And soon, we were talking on the phone just to keep each other updated on our lives. Ron was funny and smart.

Once, I had to bring the kids with me, and I decided it was time they met Ron anyway. As we drove to the church in Elon, I explained to them that Ronald had spent time in prison because I had thought he'd done a bad thing, but that I had been wrong. The kids were absolutely fascinated with him.

"What was prison like?" Blake, the bravest, asked.

"Well, it was tough. The food wasn't very good, for one." Ron said. "But sometimes we found ways to have things that reminded us of home."

"Like what?"

"Well, did you know that you can make chocolate milk with M&M's?" he said.

"You can?" they said in wide-eyed unison.

"Yup. I'd take a whole bunch of toilet paper and wrap it around and around in my hand real tight, in the shape of an *O*. If you don't wrap it tight enough, it burns too fast. Then you fill an empty milk carton with water, and you push the end of a clothes hanger through the spout, so you can hang the carton off it. I'd put the toilet paper on the back of the commode and light it on fire, holding the carton over it to warm up the water. Then when the water is warm, you dump in some M&M's and stir them around until they melt. You put as much in as you want until it tastes the way you want it," Ron explained.

After the photographer took our picture, Ronald said, "I'm going over to meet Tom at B. Christopher's for lunch. Y'all want to come?"

The kids looked at me. "Please, please!" they said. "Please, can we go?" I said we could.

Then Blake suddenly blurted out, "Can I ride in your truck, Mr. Cotton?"

Ron looked at me, and Blake, remembering he had a mother, looked at me, too.

"If it's OK with your mother," Ron said.

"Wear your seatbelt," I told Blake.

And there it was: my only son riding in a sky-high truck with Ronald Cotton. I didn't even think about it until after the fact: I trusted Ronald with my child's life.

· · ·

Rob Johnson called me one day to ask if I might want to give a talk at a prosecutorial symposium he was teaching in Asheville, North Carolina. They were going to present all the facts of the case as if it were hypothetical, and then Rob wanted me to come out and speak to everyone, and reveal that the case was real. It was the first time I ever spoke in front of a group like that—speaking in front of the camera for PBS and for reporters was different, because I never got to see anyone's reaction. Despite my nerves, the looks on people's faces told me that it was so important to keep doing what I was doing. And where it once humiliated me to talk about what happened to me, every time I stood up and talked about it meant that the hour in the dark I spent with Bobby Poole had less and less of a hold on me.

CHAPTER 18

Ronald

IN AUGUST 1997, I put on my gray suit again and Robbin and I went to the capitol building in Raleigh. Governor Hunt signed a new compensation bill, entitling me to $10,000 a year for every year I spent wrongfully incarcerated. I was very touched when Tom showed me that Jennifer Thompson, Rob Johnson, and Mike Gauldin had all written in letters on my behalf.

Once the bill became law, everybody thought it meant I'd get $110,000, because it had been eleven long years. But until Tom made a big stink, they tried to say that it was only ten years and 164 days; the half year I spent in Alamance County Jail awaiting trial didn't count to them, so they only wanted to pay up $105,000. In the end, Tom appealed the decision and the state paid me $109,150.69. No rounding up, despite all that talk that you can't put a price on a man's life. Tom also straightened things out when

I got a notice claiming I owed $5,000 in back pay to my court-appointed attorneys.

With the money from the compensation award, Robbin and I bought land in Mebane, a small town just outside Burlington. The lot we found sat at a dead end, surrounded by plenty of wide-open space. It felt secluded, and we could set a house way back from the road. That way, we wouldn't have to worry about kids running out into the street, which was very important. Robbin was pregnant.

We bought a modular home, a four-bedroom plan that would be built in a factory, and then, once the land had been cleared and a foundation poured, set into the foundation. It took longer than they told us it would—they were always blaming the weather—but eventually, our house was in. It was a ranch house with beige siding and red shutters. When it was warm, I liked to just sit outside in a chair, looking at the trees—we had apple, mulberry, and persimmon trees, and even a muscadine bush on the property—and listen to the quiet.

. . .

I took a new job at a plant where I could get a late shift, because I could make more money that way. Sometimes, before heading home, I'd drive around. I even found a bar in Burlington where people could sing karaoke. The first time I got up to sing, I wondered why I had thought it was a good idea, everyone just staring at me over their beers. But once I started singing the words to Lionel Richie's "Hello," and the crowd cheered, I stopped being nervous. Singing a few songs helped me unwind from working, and then I'd drive home and sit in my reclining chair, watching TV and unwind some more. Robbin would be fast asleep in the bedroom while I sat out in the living room. I didn't like to sleep much—life just seemed too short. One evening, I was sitting there watching a movie—they usually ran action movies and horror movies late at night—when Robbin came running out of the bedroom.

"Ron! My water broke!"

We packed up her stuff and got in the car to go to the hospital. I was trying to drive carefully, but Robbin was hollering something fierce. As we approached the intersection of South Mebane and Chapel Hill roads, the light turned red.

"Run it!" she yelled, as I began slowing down the car.

It was the middle of the night, but I couldn't do it. I didn't want us to get T-boned in the intersection—and you never knew what cops might be around, looking for drunks. I came to a complete stop, and it seemed like every second was a minute waiting for that green light. Robbin was so mad at me for not running the light.

In the delivery room, Robbin screamed. I tried holding her hand, but she kept scratching at my arm.

"This is your fault!" she said. "It's all your fault!"

I wanted to tell her that I thought we both had something to do with it, but I knew she would have gotten even madder. So I bit my tongue and said what they told me to: "Push! Push!"

Robbin screamed until the baby's head popped out, and suddenly the doctors swooped in to get the baby, cleaning it off and clearing out its nose.

"Congratulations! You have a beautiful little girl," the nurse said, placing her in Robbin's arms.

We named her Raven, for the head full of dark hair she had, a real TWA—teeny-weeny Afro. She was long—I figured she'd be tall like me—but she was real skinny. Raven was only a little over six pounds, but she must have been maybe four pounds of lungs, because I couldn't understand how something so small could make so much noise. Just looking at her, my heart felt so full it actually hurt. I don't know who was crying more then, the baby or me.

I ran out into the hallway so I could call my family and let them know. I dialed my mother first.

"We have a baby girl, Mom. I have a daughter!"

When Raven was a few weeks old, I brought her in her car seat over to meet her grandma. My mother couldn't stop telling me how beautiful she was. "You got a beautiful daughter, Ron, bless her heart."

A few short years later, it would be my mother that I'd be carrying like a baby. Unable to walk anymore, I would bend down and tell her to put her arms around my neck, but not too tight, even though she was scared.

"Flat! You're going to hurt your back. You're going to hurt it."

"I'm not going to drop you, Mom. Don't you worry about that. I got a strong back. I know what I can carry."

· · ·

Robbin and I didn't have much time to cook once the baby was born, so often I went out to buy something ready-made. In Burlington, there was a little convenience store that I always seemed to be running out to. The owner, John, was a good guy I knew from way back. One afternoon, as I stood in line at John's—Robbin had asked me to pick up some egg sandwiches—I realized I was standing behind Luke Turner, the prosecutor from the second trial. I had not seen him since the day I was convicted, when he sat at the prosecutor's table wiping his tears of relief that I would be put away.

Turner was buying a pack of cigarettes.

"Can I see some ID?" John said to him.

"You know I'm old enough to buy cigarettes," Mr. Turner responded.

"Only thing I know about you is you don't know right from wrong, putting an innocent man in prison," John said.

Mr. Turner stiffened through his back, and then turned around, as if to see who could have heard what John said. And when he looked over his shoulder, there I was.

He quickly turned back around and put some money down on the counter before walking out. No apology, nothing. He simply got into his black Mercedes and sped off.

The other person who never apologized to me was Sully, the police officer who seemed to think that because I had dated white women, I had to be a rapist. A lot of people wonder why it even mattered to me, once I was free. But it did matter. I had no choice but to stand there in court and face the accusations, defend myself the best I could. I had no choice but to keep fighting and accept that God had a reason for me to go through what I had. I didn't try and escape; I earned my freedom through the courts that had incarcerated me. It only seemed fair that people who had a hand in putting me there should have to face what they had done.

•   •   •

After meeting Jennifer, I never really thought we'd talk again. I guess I was simply going for closure that day in the church. I was glad there were no hard feelings between us, and I hoped she would go on to have a good life. We both had to start over, in a way.

So I was surprised to hear her small voice on the line not long after. The first time she called, she just told me about some media requests she had been getting. She wanted to let me know that she wouldn't do anything without my consent, because she felt like it wasn't something that just happened to her, it happened to both of us.

Sometimes, I was able to meet her for an interview, but most of the time, I was too busy working or helping raise Raven. It got to where we talked on the phone very often. She was easy to talk to. Eventually, my heart adjusted to where I thought of her as a friend. I knew she was still coping, still struggling to forgive herself. I could hear it in her voice.

One time, I did go with her up to Seattle. We were going to do a TV show and a magazine interview, and I was very excited about seeing Seattle. We arranged it so I could get off work and Robbin's mom would watch Raven when Robbin was working. I flew from Raleigh by myself, and felt very fancy when they had a driver at the airport waiting to pick me up with a sign that read, "Mr. Cotton." He held it in front of him just like the card I had held in front of me during the lineup. Jennifer arrived at the hotel a bit later than me; she had flown in from Greensboro. After I brought up my bag to my room and unpacked, I went down to wait for her in the lobby.

We were both very nervous about being alone together for the first time. Before, the kids, or Vinny, or Robbin, or Mike—someone had always been with us.

When she arrived, she told me she was going to put her stuff in the room and then she wanted to take a long walk to stretch her legs.

"It's how I like to see things, when I travel, I walk," she said. "I walk and I walk."

I nodded. Then she said, "Would you like to come with me?"

"Sure," I said.

Jennifer was not joking when she said, "I walk and walk." But it was good to have that time; it helped us to stop feeling strange about being away together. We went down to Pike's Market, and we watched the fisherman throwing fish. One took a big old salmon and it whipped right by Jennifer's head. She screamed and I just busted up laughing. We walked so much that all of a sudden the sun had set, and I guess we didn't pay enough attention to where we were going. A feeling went through me, and ahead of us, a group of guys stood like something was going down—maybe a drug deal or something. It was not a good situation, here on this dark street. Jennifer turned to look at me. Her smile was gone and she was full of fear. I pulled her around by the elbow so she'd be on the inside of me, not on the outside. "Let's cross here," I said.

We walked quickly and silently back toward the main streets and once we got in the safer area near our hotel, Jennifer said to me, "I was really scared back there."

"Don't you know I'd never let anyone harm a hair on your head?" I told her.

Later that evening, the TV show had arranged for us to go to dinner out on the water. A limo even picked us up and brought us to a very fancy restaurant where they had made reservations for us. When we got there, the waiter kept smiling at us like we were on some big romantic date. He looked at me and said stuff like, "Would the lady like more wine?" Finally Jennifer couldn't hold it in. "Can you imagine if we told him who we were?" We both got a good laugh out of that. I think if we told our waiter, he'd have dropped our dinner plates all over the floor.

Later that night, Jennifer rung me up in my room to say she had forgotten her toothpaste. I told her to come on down and use mine. And for the rest of the trip, she came to use my Colgate twice a day. Every time she came down, I happened to be ironing.

"Do you iron everything?" she said.

I told her I did.

"Even jeans?"

"I like to look neat," I said, shrugging.

The next day, after our interview, Jennifer asked if I wanted to go to see the Space Needle. We went there and rode up to the top, and stood out on the observation deck looking at the city we had walked all over the day before. My feet were still sore, but my heart was very happy.

• • •

Every year to this day, Tom calls me up on June 30 to wish me a happy anniversary. "Another year of freedom," he says. Other than when I'm driving, I don't try to look too far ahead, and once I got out, I never wanted to look back. Only after many years had passed was I able to see the long road I had traveled—all the changes that I had made—some good and some bad. I made many wrong steps. I'm still trying to make it, and my feet hurt every day from all that walking. As long as I kept on moving forward, I knew I'd be OK. But Jennifer couldn't stop looking back.

She wanted some kind of closure by meeting with Bobby Poole, but from my experience with him, I don't think it would have helped her. I had looked into his eyes and asked him directly if he had anything to do with the crimes. He had sat on the witness stand, with the two women he had raped sitting right there in the courtroom and me sitting at the other table, and denied everything. He was a liar, pure and simple, and I think even if he'd granted her request for a meeting, he would have lied to her face. She would have found his eyes empty, like the dead man he nearly was.

Because of Bobby Poole, we were probably the only people in each other's lives who could really understand what it felt to know he would have gone to his grave with his lies. We didn't mean anything to him until the DNA nailed him. So when I read in the local paper that Bobby Poole died, I cut it out so I could send it to Jennifer. It wasn't closure, but it was an ending.

Oct. 14, 1999
2:33 P.M.

Hi Jennifer,

I pray that this brief letter reaches you and your family in good health, as well as good spirits.

As for myself, well, I can't complain. For my family, we're doing wonderful and I really feel blessed to have such a family as I do.

I've enclosed the copy of the obituary of Bobby Leon Poole that I told you I'd send.

I hope now that life will be more at ease for you and you can free your mind from the many things that bother you about this case.

I wish you and your family the best.

I'm out of here.

God bless you & your family.

Sincerely,
Ronald Cotton

CHAPTER 19

Jennifer

I KNEW BOBBY POOLE had died, but to see it there, in black and white, made it tangible. The news clip Ron sent me was just a few inches big. It actually made me sad. That at the end of this man's life, all that could be written about him was that he was an inmate at Central Prison who had died of cancer at UNC–Chapel Hill Hospital. Maybe I felt something like compassion, something I could only feel because I was a mother now. Bobby Poole had been somebody's baby once. What had happened in his life? Who was he? Sometimes I still woke from sleep with a face haunting me, but the face was scrubbed of features.

The love I had for my children was everything: There was nothing I wouldn't risk for them. I started thinking about all the children out there in the world who didn't have that kind of love. I needed to do something, so I volunteered with SCAN (Stop Child Abuse Now). "What would you like to do?" the woman asked when I called, telling me about all the programs. I told her to put me where I was needed most, wherever no one else wanted to go.

I became a lay therapist, a kind of parent aide trained to go into the homes of high-risk families who had either been court-ordered to participate in the program or had taken it upon themselves to reach out for help. I signed on with families for two to three years, trying to "reparent" the parents—help the parents learn different techniques of coping with their children, ways to discipline them that weren't emotionally or physically injuring. It was extremely difficult. At times, the family situations I walked into were incredibly dysfunctional. But what I saw completely knocked me from my moral high ground. It was way too easy, before I started working with those families, to judge them. It became very clear that parents who abuse their kids had been abused themselves. They were carrying the pain.

I worked with SCAN for about four years. It helped me to stop seeing Bobby Poole as simply "evil." In my gut, I felt that someone somewhere had failed him. So his death, while it marked an end for both Ron and myself, made me sad. But at the same time, it wasn't fair that he had gotten off this easy. Bobby Poole owed me, and he owed Ron, and he owed all the other women he had hurt. I picked up the phone and called Ron, the only other person who would understand the conflicting emotions I felt over Poole's death.

• • •

Ron and I were invited to Wake Forest University to talk about our case in connection with an event about a wrongfully convicted man named Alfred Rivera. Ron said he was hoping Robbin would come and bring the baby. Ron had talked about Raven quite a bit;

I loved hearing him tell me about what his life was like since becoming a father.

It was a gorgeous fall day, and I saw the three of them from a distance, standing in front of the doorway to the auditorium. Ron held the baby while Robbin wiped her face. When I reached them, I stood there staring at Raven and unable to speak.

"Do you want to hold her?" Robbin said.

I nodded, and took Raven from Ron's arms. She smiled at me with a beautiful dimpled smile just like her father's and grasped my hand with her tiny fingers. I held her close to me and began to sob. Holding Ron's child was one of the most profound moments of my life, because I was keenly aware that if the evidence had been lost, Ron would still be in prison. Raven, this other miracle of DNA, would have never been born.

Later, when it was my turn to speak, I stood at the podium and found Ron and his family in the audience. My eyes met Ron's, and I could scarcely get out the words. It pained me to describe Ron as I had once thought of him. For so many years, the police officers and the prosecutors told me I was the "best witness" they ever put on the stand; I was "textbook." My words had condemned Ronald, but I could only hope now every time I spoke they could celebrate and honor him, and maybe, just maybe, help to change the system to make sure when our children grew up, mistakes like this wouldn't be made.

I started getting invited to speak all over the place, and in my travels, I met men and women who have been exonerated throughout the United States. In June of 2000, I traveled to Texas for a press conference on behalf of Gary Graham, who had been sentenced to death and would be executed later that month. I had warned the organizers before I went that I was an ardent supporter of the death penalty. They told me that was fine; they simply wanted me to come and tell my story. On the plane ride over, I looked at some of the materials on Graham's conviction for murder. The single eyewitness to identify Graham at trial said she saw the killer through her windshield for a few seconds. No physical evidence linked him to the crime. I was floored. Naively, I had believed that if someone was sentenced to death, there could be no doubt about that person's guilt. But like Ron, Graham insisted he was innocent and insisted that the woman who identified him had made a mistake. I had seen my rapist for nearly a half an hour, his face had been inches from me. And yet I was completely wrong. What if this eyewitness made a deadly error?

Once I arrived in Texas, I headed out to dinner with a large group of people. After we sat down in the restaurant, the organizer suggested we introduce ourselves. One by one, twelve men and women shared their stories of being wrongfully convicted. I started perspiring and looked down. My turn came and silence fell. "Go on," the organizer encouraged me. "Tell them why you are here."

A voice that sounded like mine began talking. I told them, with no small degree of shame, that like many of them, an innocent man named Ron Cotton had lost eleven years of his life after I mistakenly identified him. "I'm sorry," I told them, although I had nothing to do with their cases. The next day, at the press conference, I openly wept and begged for clemency for Graham.

· · ·

Although Ron had helped me overcome so much, I still had a hard time forgiving myself for being less than perfect. This was not like screwing up a recipe. The mistake I made had impacted people's lives for years, and I felt it was my burden to carry. It wasn't until I heard Gary Wells, a professor from the University of Iowa, speak that I began to liberate myself from the guilt. He did a presentation about memory and eyewitness identification. It really floored me— for the first time, I understood how memory could be contaminated because of the way eyewitness evidence had been collected. Sitting in a college auditorium, I got tears in my eyes. Little did this man know, with his PowerPoint slides, that he was helping to release me.

The professor said eyewitnesses will often pick the "next best one" if the right person isn't in a lineup. Picking the wrong man had not been simply my personal failure, but a human error that many people had made and would continue to make, although he had plenty of recommendations for fixing that. One innovation he talked about was double-blind testing, where the law enforcement officer showing a lineup, like the witness, has no idea who the suspect is and therefore can't give any verbal or nonverbal clues as to whether you've picked the "right" person.

All those years ago, Mike was doing his job by the book—but when I asked him if I did OK and he told me yes, then I subconsciously tried to pick the same person out of the physical lineup. Ron was the only person who had been in both the photo and the physical lineups, making his face more familiar to me. And then the police told me I had identified the same person in the physical lineup whose photo I had selected, so by the time I went into court, everything added up for me: I was defiantly confident that Ronald Cotton was the one. My memory of the night, while vivid and visceral, was not like a VCR recording I could play at will. Seeing Ronald Cotton's face in the lineup, and in court, meant that his face eventually just replaced the original image of my attacker.

In the law books they call it "unconscious tranference;" in layman's terms, my memory had been contaminated. Later, when I looked at the composite we created and at a mug shot of Poole, I thought I had actually done a great job. The problem was that Bobby Poole had not been in my lineup; Ronald Cotton had, and at the time Ronald Cotton most resembled that composite. The standard way eyewitness evidence was collected had failed me, and because of that, I'd failed, too.

. . .

Ron and I lived about an hour and an half apart, but whenever we had a reason to be in each other's area, we would get together. Once, he and Raven had driven into Winston-Salem, and we made a plan to meet at Reynolda Gardens. Raven was probably about six by then, and she was a total daddy's girl. Ron and I sat on the bench talking, and Raven, as full of energy as any six-year-old, was running around. On a small incline, she slipped on the grass and fell.

Ron called her over sternly, and she looked down at her sneakers. He fixed the barrette that had been falling from her hair.

"Quit playing so rough. You go tearing up your clothes and your mom's going to be mad at both of us," he said. She sat down on the bench next to me, trying to behave. But you could tell she was bored silly. After a few minutes, she said, "Daddy, can I go play now?"

"Just sit here, Raven."

Raven looked to me for help. "Daddy's being mean to me," she said.

"Ron, don't be mean to her!"

He laughed.

"Kids will be kids," I said.

"Yeah, I guess you're right." He turned to Raven. "Be more careful." And with that, she took off. While she was off playing, Ron mentioned he had seen Mary Reynolds, the second victim.

"Raven was with me, you know she always wants to be with Daddy. I had to go to the mall to go to Foot Locker, 'cause a lot of stores don't carry my size."

"Why, what size are you?" I asked.

"Fourteen or fifteen," he said, somewhat sheepishly.

I looked down at his feet to check for myself, and laughed.

"Got to keep my foundation level, you know?" he replied.

"Anyway, Raven, she wanted a cookie, so we went over and were looking down at the cookies through the display case and she picked out an M&M chip cookie. I stood up to order, and there she was, Mary. She was working there, behind the counter.

"She just had this stunned look on her face, like she was seeing a ghost or something. She had aged some. She had on different glasses than what she wore in court all those years ago. But it was her. She handed me the cookie all wrapped in waxed paper, and I paid my dollar and some change."

"Did you say anything?"

"No. I just paid and walked away."

"Did she say anything?"

"Just 'thank you,' when I paid."

We both turned to watch Raven, playing carefree and easy. I knew that if I had never picked Ron, Mary would have never picked him, either.

I told Ron I thought about Mary often—almost every time I went to speak, because almost everywhere I went, there were women in the audience who have been raped. Some of them, I can spot from a mile away. Once, I had gone to speak at a Catholic church in Raleigh. It was Lent, and there were maybe about a hundred people gathered on a spring evening in the fellowship hall. I was there, of course, to talk about the empowerment that comes with forgiveness. There was a woman who sat in the front row, next to what I assumed was her husband, who held his hand over hers very affectionately. I would talk and sweep the room, making brief eye contact with different people, but every time my eyes found hers, I just knew.

Afterward, she came up to me and asked if she might speak with me a moment.

"Of course," I told her, and we moved over to a corner where we could have some privacy.

She was shaking visibly, and told me my talk had moved her, because when she was young, a family member had raped her repeatedly.

"I've never really been able to move forward," she continued. "I have a lot of difficulty accepting love, but the hardest thing is I just can't forgive myself."

"What do you mean?" I asked. "Why do you need to forgive yourself?"

"I must have done something to deserve it. I must have been an awful child, or something, or God wouldn't have punished me like that."

I felt my eyes struggling to contain the tears that had formed. "Who told you that? Why would you think that?"

"Because God punishes the sinful. I must have been being punished."

I put my arms around her and said, "You must not be praying

to my God. My God would never punish anyone in that way, especially not a child. Nothing you did made you deserve that. Nothing."

I spoke with her a few more moments, and asked her if it would be all right if I called over the priest who had helped arrange my speaking engagement to talk to her about getting some counseling.

The whole drive home, I couldn't stop thinking about her. How many women still feel that way? And even if a sexual assault victim gets the opportunity to prosecute, the defense asks questions like, "Were you drinking? What time were you out?" No wonder so many women do not prosecute, with their lives opened up like wounds. For some, the only way is to bury it. They do their best to pretend it never happened.

· · ·

Even when Ron and I weren't able to see each other, we spoke on the phone pretty often. One day I was in the kitchen fixing lunch for Brittany and Morgan, who were probably about fourteen. Ron had called me up to talk. He started in the way many of our conversations do: a simple taking stock of the smallest moments and the found beauty that comes with surviving. "I got up this morning, made some bacon and eggs, and got Raven ready to go to her grandma's house. When I came home, I was out in the yard feeding the dogs and I thought it was a beautiful day. And then you came into my mind real strong and I wondered how you were doing on this beautiful day."

"I'm doing well. Just feeding two growing girls," I said.

We chatted for a good ten minutes, and then he said, "Well, I know you got things to do and places to be. You have a blessed day. Love you."

"Love you, too," I said, and hung up.

Brittany and Morgan looked at each other with confused faces and then looked at me.

"Who was that?" Morgan asked.

"Ron," I said.

"Ron? Ron Cotton?" Brittany said. "You said you loved him?"

"Yes."

"Did he say he loves you?" Morgan asked.

"Yes, he did."

They looked at each other, their fourteen-year-old eyes huge with disbelief.

"Mom, that's really weird."

I looked at them and laughed, "Yeah, I guess it is."

It was difficult to explain to teenagers how strange life could be. Ron and I would always be connected by what had happened, and after all this time, to say we were friends just wasn't enough.

• • •

In October 2007, I invited Ron to come with me to Savannah, Georgia, where there was a march in support of Troy Anthony Davis, a man on death row. As in our case, Troy Davis was convicted mostly due to the strength of eyewitness testimony, with scant physical evidence, and there were a lot of things that troubled me about it. Amnesty International asked if I would come speak, and as I always do, I called Ron to see if he could join me. My daughter Brittany, then seventeen, would be coming, so I asked him if maybe Robbin and Raven might want to come, too.

Robbin, Raven, and Ron drove to my house in Winston-Salem and left their car parked in my driveway. Everyone piled into my

Hyundai, Ron packing himself up like a lawn folding chair for the six-hour drive. His hair was much shorter than usual—and he wore army fatigue pants.

"What're you, enlisting?" I joked with him, looking at his almost-shaven head.

"Aw, the buzzer slipped, and I nicked myself in the back."

"So he had to shave it all off!" Raven said, giggling.

On our drive down, I learned that Ron had high blood pressure, and I also learned, thanks to his wife, that Ron was not very good about taking his pills. Part of the drive through Charlotte traffic turned into a "take your pill" campaign, with Robbin, Raven, Brittany, and me all chiming in.

"I don't want anything happening to you," I said, looking at him in the passenger seat next to me. I told him about a nightmare I had just a few months ago.

"I woke up and Vinny asked me if I had a bad dream. He said he thought I was crying in my sleep. So I lay there for a few minutes, and then I remembered. I dreamt you had died, Ron, and no one told me until after. It was like four days later when I found out, so it was too late. I had missed your funeral. I was so devastated. Because I promise you I'll always be there," I said.

"Don't worry, nothing's gonna happen to me. I'm tough," he responded, making a gesture as if he was the Incredible Hulk to push through the heaviness of the moment.

After fiddling with the radio for a while, he asked me if he could pop in a CD of one of his favorite songs, "Never Give Up," by Yolanda Adams.

"Raven, you going to sing along with me?" Ron asked his daughter, who looked at him bashfully. "C'mon, we've been practicing.

You know the words," he said to her, "and you got a better voice than me."

Ron's beautiful tenor voice filled the car, and eventually Raven joined in.

I thought about how he had sung so many years ago that day in the courtroom, and how it had made me feel sick. And here he was, in my car with his wife and daughter, and his singing filled me with pure joy.

The next day, about two hundred people gathered in the parking lot of the Bolton Street Baptist Church, where the first civil rights mass meetings were held in the sixties. There were people holding banners from the NAACP, organizers from the ACLU, Amnesty, and various local church groups. For October, it was extremely warm and bright. I wore sunglasses, and at times, Ron took the sign he was carrying and held it so it would grant him some shade. All along the route, Troy Davis's sister, Martina Correia, made sure the marchers stayed hydrated by passing out cold bottles of water. We marched up Martin Luther King Jr. Boulevard, formerly West Broad Street.

Brittany marched alongside Raven. They followed in our footsteps, chanting in the call-response:

Innocence . . . !
. . . Matters!
Equal . . . !
. . . Justice!

We passed barber shops and the Civil Rights Museum, just before bearing right at Montgomery Avenue, and ending up at the new Chatham County Courthouse and Jail, where Troy Davis had been tried and convicted. Ron and I were invited up.

I took the megaphone, with Ron standing next to me like the gentle giant he is, and began:

My name is Jennifer Thompson-Cannino. In 1984, I was a college student, twenty-two years old, and was brutally raped at knifepoint in my apartment. During the attack, I made a very concerted effort to pay attention to the facial features and anything I could remember to bring to the police department later on, hoping that I would survive. A few hours later, as I was sitting in the police department, it became very clear that I had gotten a very good look at the man who had raped me. And I hated this man with a vengeance and a blind hate that I can't even articulate.

Within a few days we had a suspect, the composite sketch went out in the newspapers and one name popped up. And that name was Ronald Cotton. Under photo identification, I was able to identify my attacker and it was Ronald Cotton. Ronald Cotton was then brought into a physical lineup a few days after that, and once again, I picked Ronald Cotton. Ronald Cotton stood trial in 1985 in Alamance County in Burlington, North Carolina. It was a trial for his life. Ronald Cotton was found guilty of first-degree rape, first-degree sexual offense, and first-degree breaking and entering, and he was given life plus fifty years.

Two years later, the appellate court overturned the decision and we went back to court, and again Ronald Cotton was tried. This time he was found guilty of two rapes. Ronald Cotton was convicted, sentenced to two life sentences and fifty-four years. Ronald Cotton was never coming out of prison. And we toasted the judicial system at the DA's office, because it worked for the victim. The bad guy was going to prison forever. Never ever to be free again, never to find love, never to have children.

In 1995, a DNA test was run and when it came back, it concluded that Ronald Cotton had never been my attacker. It was a man already in prison named Bobby Poole, a man who had been brought before me in 1987 under voir dire, and I completely did not recognize him. Bobby Poole died a few years later after Ronald Cotton had come out of prison after serving eleven years. Over four thousand days, Ronald Cotton was in prison; over four thousand days, Ronald wasn't with his mother; four thousand days, he wasn't with his family. Ronald Cotton came out in 1995—June 30—and I was afraid of Ron. Two years later, I got the nerve—I don't even know if it's nerve—to see Ronald Cotton and ask him for forgiveness. And I said Ronald, "If I spent every second of every minute or every hour of every day for the rest of my life telling you how sorry I am, it wouldn't come close to how sorry I am. How I feel in my heart."

And Ronald Cotton, because he is the man he is, without blinking, took my hands, cried, and said "I forgive you. I've never hated you and I want you to be happy." Ronald Cotton and I are good friends now—since 1997. We travel around the country, we've gone to Canada, done many interviews, and are currently working on a book together. Ronald Cotton is my friend. Ronald Cotton is standing right here to my left. Please everybody, give him a big hand . . .

Ron ran his hand over his face, collecting his thoughts for a moment before he spoke to the crowd.

Good afternoon, everybody. I should say, once again, my name is Ronald Cotton. It's a pleasure and an honor to be standing before you here today. I'm quite sure you all are aware of the tragic situation pertaining to Troy Davis. I have walked somewhat in his shoes, to a certain degree, and if the crime had been committed in the seventies, I would have been on death row. I thank God it didn't happen that way. And I thank God for DNA to release me from the situation that I was in. And I admit, sometimes it gets very emotional to stand before you all after listening to Jennifer speak, because it touches me so, deep down inside. . . . But I'm just glad to be here today. And I'm glad that you all have come together as one to stand up for Troy Davis, to put your foot down to keep going forward and fight fire with fire. And so, that's all I can say right now.

We put our arms around each other, the crowd cheering, and walked back over to where Robbin, Brittany, and Raven stood. Later that night, we crossed the steep steps to head down to a restaurant on the riverwalk. And while we goofed around, I said the thing I could only say to him, knowing he would understand: "Thank God I picked you." He smiled and said, "I know what you mean." And after dinner, all of us went on a tour searching for ghosts in Savannah.

• • •

A few months after we got back to North Carolina, Tom Lambeth asked Ron and me to come to the criminal law class he teaches at my alma mater, Elon College. His class studied our case, and we went in at the end of the semester so the students could do a question-and-answer session. Rich Rosen was supposed to come, too, but he had a meeting about another postconviction case he was working on and wasn't able to make it. But Rich's son Lochlin, a freshman there, sat in the audience. At eighteen years old, he had already organized a forum on wrongful convictions.

After we finished speaking to the students, Ron and I stood in the parking lot, saying good-bye. Something caught his eye.

"You need air," he said, leaning down to look at my tires. "Your tires are low."

"You know, I thought they seemed a bit low this morning. Is there a gas station around here that could do it?"

"There's one on Church near Forty," he said.

We hugged each other good-bye and wished each other happy holidays. Then I got in my VW bug and pulled out of the parking lot. As I headed down West Front Street, I spotted a young girl walking with her backpack on, and remembered myself, at twenty-two years old, walking this way to school every day. I was so determined, so sure, and so utterly unaware of the way the road was going to twist and turn.

When I turned onto Church Street, I glanced in my rearview mirror, and noticed there was someone following me. Ron.

I pulled into the Exxon gas station and a minute later, Ron parked his brown Ford pickup beside me. He hopped out of his truck, insistent on filling my tires himself.

Once he was satisfied that my tires were full, he climbed back into his truck. He tooted his horn and leaned out his open window.

"Get home safe," he called, waving as he rolled out.

Afterword

AS OF THIS WRITING, 223 people in the United States have had their convictions overturned by DNA evidence; Ronald Cotton was number twenty-three. Over 75 percent of these cases involved mistaken eyewitness testimony, making it the leading cause of wrongful conviction. (Source: The Innocence Project)

One of those overturned convictions was Darryl Hunt, Jr., who was arrested in 1984 for the rape and murder of **Deborah Sykes,** which occurred two weeks after Jennifer Thompson's assault. Convicted in Forsyth County, North Carolina, in 1985, Darryl Hunt had DNA evidence prove his innocence in 1994, although it would take another ten years of legal appeals before Hunt was exonerated.

Ronald Cotton was the first postconviction DNA exoneree in North Carolina. His case helped establish measures for the five others in the state—to date—who have been exonerated since his release. When Ron was freed, Tom Lambeth and others worked to get a bill passed that would entitle him to $10,000 for every year he spent erroneously incarcerated, pro-rated. In 2001, the amount was increased to $20,000 per year, though it was not made retroactive.

In August of 2008, Gov. Mike Easley of North Carolina signed another change to the compensation statute: Those who received a pardon of innocence on or after January 1, 2004, could receive $50,000 for each year of wrongful imprisonment, with a cap of $750,000. Other services, such as state-funded education benefits and up to a year of job-skills training, could be included in the maximum. Ronald Cotton was granted a pardon of innocence on July 12, 1995 and thus did not qualify for the retroactive increase in compensation, tuition expenses, or job-training benefits.

For the nearly eleven years of his life lost to the wrongful conviction, Ronald Cotton received $109,150.69. (He received about $106,000 in 1997; the remaining funds were turned over to him in 2000.)

Michael R. Gauldin, the lead detective on Jennifer Thompson's case, retired as chief of police in Burlington, North Carolina, in August 2007. Under his leadership, the Burlington Police Department became the first in the state of North Carolina to mandate sequential lineups (where witnesses are shown suspects or suspects' photos one at a time, instead of simultaneously) and double-blind procedures, where the lineup administrator is not the investigating officer and therefore does not know which picture (or person, in a physical lineup) is the suspect and thus cannot provide any unintentional clues.

Robert F. Johnson, the prosecutor who oversaw Ronald's exoneration hearing, is currently the chief district attorney in Burlington, North Carolina.

D. Thomas Lambeth, Jr., the Burlington attorney who worked pro bono for Ron's release, was appointed by Governor Mike Easley to the District Court bench in the 15A Judicial District of Alamance County. After being sworn in as a district court judge on August 30, 2007, in front of friends and colleagues, including Ronald and Robbin Cotton, Jim Roberson, Rob Johnson, and Phil Moseley, he served ice cream from Smitty's Ice Cream Shop, the shop he co-owns. It was his forty-eighth birthday.

Daniel H. Monroe, Jr., who helped represent Ron in the '85 and '87 trials, is a criminal defense attorney in Graham, North Carolina.

W. Phillip Moseley, Jr., Ron's court-appointed attorney from the '85 and '87 trials, is in general practice in Burlington, North Carolina. Phil had called Dr. Reed Hunt, a memory expert, to testify for the defense in both trials. The juries were not allowed to hear Dr. Hunt's testimony in either trial. From 1998 to 2006, Phil Moseley and Tom Lambeth worked at the same practice in downtown Burlington.

Richard A. Rosen, the law professor who took on Ron's case and helped win his freedom, oversaw the clinical programs at UNC–Chapel Hill Law School until 2008, when he retired after more than twenty years teaching. Following Ronald's exoneration, Rich was so deluged with letters from people asking for help with their cases that he started an Innocence Project with his students. To better coordinate the efforts of Innocence Projects at UNC–Chapel Hill, Duke University, and other North Carolina schools, the North Carolina Center on Actual Innocence was incorporated as a nonprofit in 2000. One of Rich's former students, Christine Mumma, started with the Center in 2001.

In 2002, through Christine Mumma's efforts, the North Carolina Actual Innocence Commission (now called the North Carolina Chief Justice's Study Commission), was established by former Chief Justice I. Beverly Lake. Mike Gauldin, Rob Johnson, and Rich Rosen were initial members; Jennifer Thompson-Cannino joined in 2003. The Innocence Commission studied postconviction review processes for innocence claims and made recommendations for improving the system. From their recommendations, North Carolina passed legislation in 2006 to establish the Innocence Inquiry Commission, the country's first formal state agency designed to be an independent truth-seeking forum for justice in innocence cases.

In 2008, Rich received the Thomas Paine Award from the Common Sense Foundation, a North Carolina public policy organization that promotes equality and justice. Jennifer and Ron spoke at the ceremony.

Troy Anthony Davis was sentenced to death in 1991 for the murder of Savannah police officer Mark Allen MacPhail, though no physical evidence linked him to the crime. Since Davis's conviction, seven state witnesses—including five eyewitnesses—have recanted portions of their testimony, and some have alleged police coercion.

Another man implicated in the murder, Sylvester "Redd" Coles, was not investigated.

In March 2008, the Georgia Supreme Court ruled 4–3 against Davis's bid for a new trial. The U.S. Supreme Court stayed Davis's execution in September 2008, just hours before he was scheduled to die. However, because of restrictions on Federal appeals processes, the Supreme Court ultimately denied Davis's request for a hearing to determine the reliability of the eyewitness evidence used to convict him. At the time this book was going to press, the 11th Circuit Court of Appeals in Atlanta agreed to consider whether or not Davis should be permitted further appeals. Davis has always maintained his innocence.

A Note on Sources

THIS BOOK IS BASED on Jennifer's and Ronald's recollections, aided in part by notes, letters, and other personal documents. Writing a book about events spanning nearly twenty-five years—especially one whose subtext is the fallibility of memory itself—posed an inherent challenge. Interviews with the following individuals, among others, greatly helped in clarifying events and they are quoted throughout the book as re-imagined conversations: Janet Thompson Barnard, Marietta (Tudy) Bruce, Robbin Cotton, Michael (Mike) R. Gauldin, Robert (Rob) F. Johnson, D. Thomas (Tom) Lambeth, Jr., W. Phillip (Phil) Moseley, Jr., Daniel (Dan) H. Monroe, Jr., James (Jim) K. Roberson, Richard (Rich) A. Rosen, Rowena (Diane) D. Shavers, Alameda Wheeler, Shelia (Pig) Wheeler, Terry H. Wheeler, and "Sadie."

Much of the written record exists and was reviewed. We relied most heavily on the Burlington Police Department's investigation file, North Carolina Internal Records OCA Number 8427581, graciously provided by Mike Gauldin; transcripts for the first trial in January, 1985, taken from the record of the North Carolina Supreme Court case, *State of North Carolina v. Ronald Junior Cotton*, 318 N.C. 663 (1987); and transcripts for the second trial in November 1987, taken from the record of the North Carolina Supreme Court case, *State of North Carolina v. Ronald Junior Cotton*, 329 N.C. 764 (1991).

Ronald's fight to have the 170 days he spent in Alamance County Jail count in the Award of Compensation granted to him by the state of North Carolina (N.C. Gen. Statute §148–84) was detailed in the document N.C. Industrial Commission No. EC000003, *Ronald Junior Cotton, Claimant v. N.C. Department of Correction, Defendant*, opinion and award filed July 31, 2000.

Letters excerpted herein are actual letters; no words were changed though omissions were made to protect the privacy of other individuals. In a few instances, letters were used as the basis to reconstruct phone conversations. Much of the correspondence in this book and the documentation concerning the motion for appropriate relief come from the files of Rich Rosen.

Facts about the Deborah Sykes case came from the excellent and comprehensive investigative series "Murder, Race, & Justice: The State v. Darryl Hunt" done by *The Winston-Salem Journal* and available at http://darrylhunt.journalnow.com/frontStories.html.

"What Jennifer Saw" was written, produced, and directed by Ben Loeterman. It aired on PBS's *Frontline* on February 25, 1997.

Quotes from the *Larry King Live* show are taken from Ronald Cotton's appearance on July 13, 1995.

Facts about the Troy Anthony Davis case come from the

Amnesty USA report " 'Where Is the Justice for Me?' The Case of Troy Anthony Davis Facing Execution in Georgia" available at http://www.amnestyusa.org/document.php?lang=e&id=ENGAMR 510232007 and "Execution of GA Man Near Despite Recantations: Some Witnesses Now Say He Is Innocent" by Peter Whoriskey, *The Washington Post*, July, 16, 2007.

Please visit our Web site, pickingcottonbook.com, for more information about some of the legal issues surrounding the *State v. Cotton*, additional photos, and a list of resources.

Acknowledgments

FOR EVERYTHING THEY DID for Jennifer and Ronald so many years ago and everything they continue to do to help them, including the time and access they gave in service of getting this book done, we owe Mike Gauldin, Rob Johnson, Tom Lambeth, Dan Monroe, Phil Moseley, Jim Roberson, Rich Rosen, and the various people who asked not to be named our deepest gratitude.

We would also like to say a special thank you to award-winning filmmaker Jessica Sanders, whose hunch about our fit was the beginning, at long last, of seeing this dream come true. We were so lucky to have Hilary Rubin Teeman as our editor. She championed the project from the beginning and her skillful insight added so much to what you hold in your hands. Tina Wexler at ICM worked tirelessly on our behalf and made sure that this book was always a priority.

Thank you: Ron Bernstein of ICM; Matt Torneo for designing our proposal cover; Louie Fleck for his photoshop help; Lisa D'Angelo and Laura Hastay for explaining various legal issues; Nick Sexton of the UNC-Chapel Hill Law Library for his invaluable research assistance; Becky Wilson of UNC-Chapel Hill for making the parking so easy; Randy Jones, Captain Brad Evans, and Captain Ricky Durham of the Alamance County Sheriff's Office; Deputy Chief of the Burlington Police, Tim Flack; Warden Marvin Polk of Central Prison in Raleigh, North Carolina; Diana Sherill, of the Burlington Police Department; Thomas Boney, Jr. of *The Alamance News*; Ben Loeterman; Michael Hirt and Towers Productions; Heather Florence; Sonny Goodnoe; Chris Mumma of the North Carolina Center on Actual Innocence; Everette Catilla of Amnesty International; John Murphy, Jason Ramirez, Stephen Lee, Dori Weintraub, Tara Cibelli, Jane Liddle, Ann Day, and everyone at St. Martin's Press for giving our book such a good home.

For their early words of support: Barry Scheck and the Innocence Project, Julia Cheffeitz, Ginny Sloan of the Constitution Project, Christine Earle, Janet Reno, and Sister Helen Prejean.

This book was supported in part by the Soros Justice Fellowship Program of the Open Society Institute. The authors gratefully acknowledge OSI's assistance, especially Adam Culbreath, Amy Weil, and Christina Voight.

From Jennifer

Thank you to the Manness Family for risking their lives by taking me in, and Mike Gauldin for keeping me from completely falling apart.

To my Mom and Dad, brothers, sister, and their families, for loving me when I was sometimes very unlovable.

Andrea, Mary, Debbie, Tami, Cindy, Lyn, Regina, and Kristine: thanks for listening to me over and over again!

To Steve McCuthan for telling me to listen to God, He will always give me the right words. Thank you!

To Larry Marshall, Rob Warden, Dick Burr, and Barry Scheck for giving me a voice to do this work.

To my children, Morgan, Blake, and Brittany, whose very presence on this earth reminds me each and every day what life is really about. I love you three more than all the . . . !

To Hennie, for being such a wonderful other mother to me.

To Vinny, for coming into my life when I needed you. Thank you.

To Ronald, thank you for teaching me about grace and forgiveness when you did not have to.

To Erin, for believing in our story and being present in our hearts.

To all the exonerees who have graced me with your stories and lives of faith, you amaze me.

To all my friends and family wherever you are, I love you more than you can possibly know and thank you for your true acts of friendship and faith.

From Ron

To my late father, who was always an inspiration and a vision of hope throughout my incarceration.

To my mother, who was always there for me, my pillar of strength.

To my lawyers, and everyone who was there helping me to "right" the injustice I endured.

To Robbin, for all her support, understanding, and guidance during my time of adjustment back into society.

To my daughter, Raven, that she might one day know the truth.

To Jennifer, for having the courage to admit her mistake.

To Erin, for being so dedicated and making the writing process so much easier, and for becoming my friend along the way.

To all my family and friends, too numerous to mention names, but you know who you are, thank you all for all that you have done for me, for standing by me, believing in me, and helping in all the ways you could.

From Erin

Thank you: Fellow writers Michelle Chihara, Jennifer Stroup Drew, Valerie Krause, Jesse Noonan, Barbara Fleck-Paladino, Loni Steele, Jennifer Stroup, and Josh Swiller for reading chapters and drafts and giving me invaluable feedback. Jen, I am eternally grateful for your incisive comments, edits, and all-around advice.

Michele Zito of David's Travel in West Hartford, Connecticut, for quickly and ably handling my ever-changing itineraries; Marisa Giardina for the unexpected trip down memory lane; Victoria Rowan and The TK Writers' Group; Donna Brodie and The Writers' Room NYC; Impact Personal Safety in Los Angeles; and The New York Foundation for the Arts.

To all my wonderful friends and family, but most especially my mother, Ann, and my husband, Sascha, whose love and support were my constant companions on this journey. They knew this was a story I had to write, and without them, I could have never taken it on.

And lastly, to Jennifer and Ron, whose strength and dignity inspire me every day. I'm lucky enough to call them my very dear friends.

About the Authors

JENNIFER THOMPSON-CANNINO lives in North Carolina with her family. She speaks frequently about the need for judicial reform, and is a member of the North Carolina Actual Innocence Commission, the advisory committee for Active Voices, the Constitution Project, and Mothers for Justice. Her op-eds have appeared in *The New York Times*, *The Durham-Herald Sun*, and *The Tallahassee Democrat*.

RONALD COTTON lives with his wife and daughter in North Carolina, and currently works at an insulation plant. He has spoken at various schools and conferences including Washington and Lee University, University of Nevada Las Vegas, Georgetown Law School, and the Community March for Justice for Troy Anthony Davis in Savannah, Georgia.

ERIN TORNEO is a writer who divides her time between Los Angeles, California, and Brooklyn, New York. She was a 2007 New York Foundation for the Arts Nonfiction Fellow.

Ronald, Jennifer, and Erin received the 2008 Soros Justice Media Fellowship for this book.